Theologies of Land

Crosscurrents in Majority World and Minority Theology

Series Editors:
K. K. Yeo and Gene L. Green

As Christianity continues to expand in the global South and East, demand has grown for thoughtful biblical and theological analysis that addresses the concerns of the Majority World as well as minority Christians in the colonial contexts. The "Crosscurrents in Majority World and Minority Theology" series attempts to harness this promising moment by addressing themes central to Majority World and minority biblical studies and theology that often find no place in North Atlantic discussions around traditional theological loci, such as land, migration, and identity. The series promotes engagement with the best resources from World Christianity, bringing the current and next generation of Majority World and Minority scholars into dialog with each other.

Theologies of Land

Contested Land, Spatial Justice, and Identity

EDITED BY

K. K. Yeo

AND

Gene L. Green

CASCADE *Books* · Eugene, Oregon

THEOLOGIES OF LAND
Contested Land, Spatial Justice, and Identity

Crosscurrents in Majority World and Minority Theology

Cascade Books
An Imprint of Wipf and Stock Publishers
199 W. 8th Ave., Suite 3
Eugene, OR 97401

www.wipfandstock.com

PAPERBACK ISBN: 978-1-7252-6506-6
HARDCOVER ISBN: 978-1-7252-6507-3
EBOOK ISBN: 978-1-7252-6508-0

Cataloguing-in-Publication data:

Names: Yeo, K. K., editor. | Green, Gene L., editor.

Title: Theologies of land : contested land, spatial justice, and identity / edited by K. K. Yeo and Gene L. Green.

Description: Eugene, OR: Cascade Books, 2021. | Crosscurrents in Majority World and Minority Theology. | Includes bibliographical references and index.

Identifiers: ISBN 978-1-7252-6506-6 (paperback). | ISBN 978-1-7252-6507-3 (hardcover). | ISBN 978-1-7252-6508-0 (ebook).

Subjects: LCSH: Bible—Hermeneutics. | Imperialism. | Arab-Israeli conflict. | Apartheid. | Indians of North America—Religion. | Liberation theology—United States. | Postcolonial theology. | Decoloniality.

Classification: BR1110 T18 2021 (print). | BR1110 (ebook).

To the Peoples of the Land

Contents

Preface

OVER A PERIOD OF six years, K. K. Yeo (Garrett-Evangelical Theological Seminary), Steve Pardue (Asia Graduate School of Theology), and Gene Green (Wheaton College and Graduate School) brought together forty biblical scholars and theologians from the Majority World, along with six Euro-American theologians, to present their reflections on the Christian faith. Each interacted with the historic creeds of the church and undertook contextualized theological work on the Christian faith, surveying developments in their regions and presenting their own constructive theology. Their joint work focused on six traditional theological loci—the doctrines of God (Trinity), christology, pneumatology, soteriology, ecclesiology, and eschatology—and their essays became the "Majority World Theology Series," now published by Langham Literature and IVP Academic (originally by Eerdmans). This monumental global series sought to further international theological dialog and encourage non-Majority World scholars and students to listen deeply to the fresh voices and developments in what Andrew Walls and Justo González called a global "new Reformation" or "macro Reformation."

During the yearly gatherings that produced the "Majority World Theology Series," an awareness grew that other theological topics required attention. These were not the traditional loci of Euro-American thought but theologies worked out in the crucible of daily life in diverse global and minority communities. The theologies did not appear in the majority of publishers' stock lists and regularly assigned theological texts, they did not find place within theological curricula, and they did not appear in most course work in biblical and theological studies. The topics were varied and vital, the stuff of a true theology on the road, that place where "life is tensely lived," as John Mackay said in his *Preface to Christian Theology*. Themes such as land, migration, identity, and others are vital human concerns that cry for theological reflection. The "Crosscurrents in Majority World and Minority Theology" series is an attempt to bring together notable biblical scholars and theologians who are undertaking critical contextual work on these and other topics. This is part of the ongoing dialog among Majority World scholars from Africa, Asia, and Latin America, and Indigenous communities alongside those from Minority communities in North America who together will soon become the majority voices in their context's theological reflection.

The first volume in the series, *Theologies of Land*, could not have come into existence without the collaboration of many committed individuals and communities. The first thanks goes to the authors in this volume. Mitri Raheb represents the Palestinian Christian community, Oscar García-Johnson from Honduras gives voice to Latin American and Latinx reflection, Cree-Anishinaabe scholar H. Daniel Zacharias represents the First Nations concerns, and Hulisani Ramantswana stands for the Christian community in South Africa. Walter Brueggemann is one of the best-known North American scholars who has written on a theology of land and honors us with his voice in the Introduction to this volume. K. K. Yeo not only drew together the varied voices in the summary Conclusion but adds his own reflection as a Chinese scholar who works at the intersection of the theologies of land and identity. We all owe a special note of thanks to the institutions they represent that helped fund the authors' participation in this global dialog.

Evan Hunter, Vice President of ScholarLeaders International, secured additional funding for the gathering, including a greatly appreciated luncheon where dialog continued. The discussion on the theologies of land took place at the 2019 meeting of the Institute of Biblical Research, an organization that has heartily supported this and previous discussions on Majority World and Minority biblical studies and theology. Two publishers have made the Crosscurrents in Majority World and Minority Theology series available to students and scholars throughout the globe. Together we offer hearty thanks to Michael Thomson of Cascade Books and Luke Lewis of Langham Literature. Thanks to Kungsiu Lau for meticulously compiling the indices. Their labors, encouragement, and patience bring us no end of joy.

Finally, *thank you, good reader*, for walking along on this journey and listening deeply. Lessons abound along this road. You will see.

Contributors

Walter Brueggemann is William Marcellus McPheeters Professor Emeritus of Old Testament at Columbia Theological Seminary. He is a past president of the Society of Biblical Literature and an ordained minister in the United Church of Christ. A prolific international writer with works translated into numerous languages, he is the world's leading interpreter of the Old Testament and is the author of numerous books, including Westminster John Knox best sellers such as *Genesis* and *First and Second Samuel* in the Interpretation series, and *An Introduction to the Old Testament: The Canon and Christian Imagination*. He has recently published *Materiality as Resistance* (Westminster John Knox, 2020), *Gift and Task* (Westminster John Knox, 2017), and *Money and Possessions* (Westminster John Knox, 2016).

Oscar García-Johnson (PhD in Theology, Fuller Theological Seminary) is Academic Dean and Associate Professor of Theology and Latino/a Studies at Fuller Theological Seminary. He has directed the Center for the Study of Hispanic Church and Community at Fuller Seminary since 2016. Born in Honduras, García-Johnson is an ordained minister with the American Baptist Churches USA, has planted four churches in Southern California and served as denominational leader for eleven years prior to coming to Fuller Seminary as a regular faculty member. His theological methodology is known as Transoccidentalism, which critically and constructively engages with Western classical theologies, Indigenous spiritualities of the South, Latino/a American Studies and theologies, and decoloniality. His writings include: *Spirit Outside the Gate: Decolonial Pneumatologies of the*

American Global South (IVP Academic, 2019), *The Mestizo/a Community of the Spirit: Toward a Postmodern Latino/a Ecclesiology* (Pickwick Publications, 2009), *Conversaciones Teológicas del Sur Global Americano: Violencia, Desplazamiento y Fe* (Puertas Abiertas/Wipf&Stock, 2016), co-edited with Milton Acosta, and *Theology without Borders: Introduction to Global Conversations* (Baker Academic, 2015), co-authored with William Dyrness. Both his wife Karla and son Christian are involved in pastoral work.

Mitri Raheb (Doctorate in Theology from the Philipps University at Marburg) is the Founder and President of Dar al-Kalima University College of Arts and Culture in Bethlehem. The most widely published Palestinian theologian to date, the Rev. Dr. Raheb is the author of twenty books including: *The Cross in Contexts: Suffering and Redemption in Palestine, I am a Palestinian Christian, Bethlehem Besieged,* and *Faith in the Face of Empire: The Bible through Palestinian Eyes.* His books and numerous articles have been translated so far into eleven languages. A social entrepreneur, Rev. Raheb has founded several NGOs including the Christian Academic Forum for Citizenship in the Arab World (CAFCAW). Dr. Raheb received in 2017 the Tolerance Award from the European Academy of Science and Arts, in 2015 the Olof Palme Prize, in 2012 the prestigious German Media Prize, in 2003 the Wittenberg Award from the Luther Center in DC and in 2007 the well-known German Peace Award of Aachen. He also received for his "outstanding contribution to Christian education through research and publication" an honorary doctorate from Concordia University in Chicago (2003) and for his interfaith work the "International Mohammad Nafi Tschelebi Peace Award" of the Central Islam Archive in Germany (2006).

Hulisani Ramantswana (PhD, Westminster Theological Seminary) is an associate professor at the University of South Africa, Department of Biblical and Ancient Studies. He earned his doctorate in the field of Hermeneutics and Biblical Interpretation, with a focus on the Old Testament. His research interests include African Biblical Hermeneutics, decolonial readings of the Bible, Pentateuch, and creation narratives. He argues for the importance of reading the Bible through our African knowledge systems and in terms of our life experiences and our life experiences in terms of the Bible. In his view, issues such as poverty, inequality, landlessness, abuse of power, xenophobia, colonial experiences, coloniality, imperialism, globalization, among others, should inform our readings of the Bible. His recent articles include: 'Wathint' Umfazi, Wanthint' Imbokodo, Uzakufa (You Strike a

Woman, You Strike a Rock, You Will Die); "Dina and Tamar as Rape Pro-
testors," *HTS Theological Journal* 75 (2019); "Song(s) of Struggle: A Decolonial Reading of Psalm 137 in Light of South Africa's Struggle Songs," *Old
Testament Essays* 32 (2019); "From Royal Tribe to Landless Tribe: Royal
Line of Levi (Moses) Broken through Young Aide," *Journal for Semitics* 26
(2017); "The Levites' Exclusion from Land Allotment: The Joshua Story in
Dialogue with the Joseph Story", *Old Testament Essays* 30 (2017); and "Be-
ware of the (Westernized) African Eyes: Rereading Psalm 82 through the
Vhufa Approach," *Scriptura* 116 (2017).

H. Daniel Zacharias (PhD, Highland Theological College/Aberdeen) is a
Cree-Anishinaabe/Austrian man from Treaty One territory in Manitoba.
He lives in Wolfville, Nova Scotia, with his wife Maria and four children
Lex, Jack, Ella-Rose, and Hudson. He serves as Associate Professor of New
Testament Studies at Acadia Divinity College in Nova Scotia, located in
the ancestral and unceded territory of the Mi'kmaq peoples. He also serves
as a faculty member with *NAIITS: An Indigenous Learning Community*.
He is ordained with the Convention of the Atlantic Baptist Churches. His
research and writing interests continue in the Gospel of Matthew, which
was the focus of his dissertation, theology of land and ecotheology, and
Indigenous Christian theologies.

Editors

K. K. Yeo (PhD, Northwestern University), is Harry R. Kendall Professor
of New Testament at Garrett-Evangelical Seminary and affiliate professor
at the Department of Asian Languages and Cultures at Northwestern University in Evanston, Illinois. He is an elected member of the Society of New
Testament Studies since 1998, also a Lilly Scholar (1999) and Henry Luce
Scholar (2003). In the last fifteen years, he has been a visiting professor to
major universities in China. He has authored or edited more than forty
Chinese and English-language books on critical engagement between Bible
and cultures, including *Musing with Confucius and Paul* (Cascade Books,
2008), *What Has Jerusalem to Do with Beijing?* (Pickwick Publications,
2018), and the editor of *The Oxford Handbook of the Bible in China* (Oxford
University Press, 2021). Yeo also co-edited the Majority World Theology
Series (Langham Literature and IVP Academic).

Gene L. Green (PhD, University of Aberdeen) is the Dean of Trinity International University–Florida and Professor Emeritus of New Testament at Wheaton College and Graduate School. Previously he served as Professor of New Testament, Academic Dean, and Rector of the Seminario ESEPA in San José, Costa Rica. He is the author of *Vox Petri: A Theology of Peter* (Cascade Books, 2019), four biblical commentaries written in Spanish and English, co-author of *The New Testament in Antiquity* (Zondervan, 2019), and co-editor of *Global Theology in Evangelical Perspective* (IVP Academic, 2012) and the Majority World Theology Series (Langham Literature and IVP Academic). His research focuses on the intersection of the Christian faith and cultures, both ancient and contemporary.

Introduction

Theologies of the Land

WALTER BRUEGGEMANN

THE FOUR STRONG ESSAYS plunge us into hard contestation concerning long assumed *colonizing truths* and new *historical possibility* beyond that long assumed normativity. One of the sites for that contestation is indeed the Bible; the Bible offers a narrative of predation that thrives on chosenness, entitlement, and God-authorized conquest. The Bible offers, alongside that narrative of *predation*, an alternative narrative of *emancipation* wherein the holy power of God is mobilized to create and authorize life outside the reach of predatory power. That contestation between predation and emancipation is surely present in the Bible itself. It is, moreover, powerfully present in the long history of biblical interpretation, a contest between those who read "from above," who have dominated Western reading (in both fundamentalist and historical-critical modes), and those who read "from below," now represented by bold, imaginative, post-colonial work. These essays reflect various specific socio-cultural contexts; in the end, however, the contestation is the same everywhere, wherein the powers of predation have the upper hand, but witnesses to and practitioners of emancipation continue the long work of subversive imagination.

Wondering how I might introduce these essays as an Old Testament teacher, I have decided that they might be read as shrewd, poignant commentary on Psalm 73. Thus I will take Psalm 73 as a map for this ongoing introduction. The Psalm is divided into two extended parts with

1

an abrupt turn in between the two parts. I will let this mapping shape my introductory comments.

I.

In Psalm 73, verses 2–14 offer self-critical reflection by one who has engaged in long-term resistance to a life of exploitative self-indulgence. I take these verses in the psalm to articulate envy of the way of the colonizing ones so well identified in these essays. The psalmist reflects on a practice of arrogance that has led to uncommon wealth, privilege, and wellbeing. Those who practice such aggressive exploitation have bodies that reflect rest, good food, comfort, and security (vv. 4–7). Their unmitigated wellbeing produces a sense of self-sufficiency that makes them immune to any accountability to God: "How can God know?" (v. 11). Their wealth and social power give them the capacity to do as they please so that they are "always at ease" with ever growing wealth (v. 12). They are shameless in their wellbeing that no doubt has resulted from sharp exploitative practices that leads to the seizure of the property of others.

By verse 13 the psalmist concludes that his/her pious practice of Torah obedience and neighborly ethics are foolish investments of attention and energy, a waste of time, all "in vain." The psalmist sees that it works better to do whatever is necessary to be on to top of the social heap, unrestrained by old-fashioned neighborly mandates. I take the words of these verses to be a fair characterization of the ruthless exploitative power of the colonizers of the West who have reduced the rest of the world and its inhabitants to disposable commodities, including for example, the Palestinians and the Black population of South Africa.

It is useful, I judge, to see that these essays reflect the same critical awareness as these verses in the psalm. Such exploitation does work . . . for some at the high cost to others. García-Johnson has seen that the long history of Western exploitation, authorized by the Papal decree of 1493, has moved through colonizing (1500–1800), Americanizing (1900), development (1930–1960), and market capitalism (1970–2000). The logic of colonizing and the rhetoric of modernity have resulted in a ruthless division of the earth and its goods between *landlords* and *the landless*. There is, moreover, no doubt that this long-term exploitative enterprise is permeated with racism, even now in the mantra of US white nationalism, "Make America Great Again." Raheb has shown how the Bible has served such predation so that even the land of the Bible (Palestine) has been endlessly occupied by exploitative powers, not least by the brutal coming of the community of Joshua at the outset. His appeal to the narrative of Naboth's vineyard is exactly to the point, where ruthless usurpatious power takes the land (inheritance!) of the vulnerable. (It should be noted that in US foreign policy, that same narrative has been a useful point of critical awareness for US preemptive aggression. In 1870 Charles Sumner in the US Senate gave a speech that was titled "Naboth's Vineyard" concerning the proposed US annexation of the island of San Domingo. In 1928 Sumner Welles, in the US State Department, wrote of *Naboth's Vineyard: The Dominican Republic 1844–1924*, again concerning rapacious US policy. Ramantswana has pursued the same prism to identify the theft of land in South Africa by the long-term occupiers. He offers a brilliant reading of how conquest works in the book of Joshua whereby the land comes to new "ownership." Zacharias has seen, moreover, that common notions of "stewardship" of the creation have been hubristic and have exalted human persons over other creatures to their great detriment and diminishment. On all these counts, the work of the occupiers has been to grab the land of the vulnerable, a point made by the prophet Micah in his exposition of the Tenth Commandment of Sinai:

> Alas for those who devise wickedness and evil deeds on their beds!
> When morning dawns, they perform it,
>> because it is in their power.
> They covet fields, and seize them;
>> houses, and take them away;
> they oppress householder and house,
>> people and their inheritance (Mic 2:1–2).

"Alas" indeed! Alas, because such exploitation is not sustainable in the long run of history where the purpose of the holy God is operative. This is a conclusion reached only slowly by the psalmist.

II.

In verses 18–28 the psalmist reflects a fresh, alert awareness of the reality of God as the psalmist has come to herself/himself (see Luke 15:17). Now the psalmist criticizes the predators that he/she has recently envied and sees that such envy was an act both "stupid and ignorant" as a dumb-ass ("brute beast," v. 21). The psalmist sees that prideful arrogance will not endure, but will vanish from the earth without a track in the sand:

> How they are destroyed in a moment,
>> swept away utterly by terrors!
> They are like a dream when one awakes;
>> on awaking you despise their phantoms. (vv. 19–20)

The point is seen so clearly by Raheb in his shrewd reading of the Beatitude. He readily observes that "empires come and go" and have no staying power. By contrast the "meek" inhabitants of the land persist and endure, and finally will have their land because it rightly belongs to them. This is a remarkable insight of affirmation that concerns Palestinians, Blacks in South Africa, and Indigenous peoples in North America and beyond. It is a lesson the US has learned the hard way in Viet Nam. Those who belong in, with, to, and for the land will not be displaced by the force and mechanisms of the ruthless confiscators who occupy.

The psalmist comes to see that the aggressiveness of the predators brings no durable safety or satisfaction. In the end what matters is close connection to the creator God who, beyond every such predation, brings the "meek" to wellbeing. It is fair to see that this connection to the creator is both *corporeal* and *dialogical*. It is *corporal* as the psalmist can speak of "flesh, heart, and hand" all linked to the creator. The psalmist has not forgotten that the creator God cares about bodily reality, even when it is not "sound and sleek" (v. 4) in a way that resists the preferred disembodied minds of colonial modernity. It is *dialogical* in that the psalmist is "with you" (v. 23). The psalmist and the creator God are "hand-in-hand" in ways that give strength to the psalmist (v. 26). This dialogical mode of life is resistance to the top-down monologic mode that is preferred by imperial power.

While the point is not explicitly voiced in the psalm, this unmistakably *dialogic* relationship between the psalmist and the creator permits us to allow that the psalm makes room for and assumes a triangular interdependence of creator, human creatures, and other non-human creatures. This mode of thought moves toward an equitable justice among the creatures and to the championing of small-time agriculture (alongside Wendell Berry) and to the rejection of agribusiness that is an expression of corporate commoditization, a part of land-grab and money-grab. Indeed the prophet Micah recognizes that when the "war economy" is terminated, it will be possible for small farmers to enjoy the produce of their own land

(Mic 4:1–4). This wondrous appreciation of creation and the capacity to enjoy it outside the reach of market commoditization lets us see the amazing interdependence of all of creation. Zacharias appreciates the reciprocity of human agents with the creator so that they may function as co-creators with God. He sees that the practice of rest for the land is an act of defiance against the unrestrained commoditization of the land under market mandates. One compelling acknowledgment of this reciprocity is voiced by Ellen Davis who affirms the long-term fruitfulness intended by the creator when the land is properly valued and tended:

> Yet, in fact, small farms everywhere, in North America and also in the Third World, are more productive than large ones, for multiple reasons . . . Plants do favors for each other. In agrarian cultures in Mexico and northern Central America, farmers have traditionally interplanted "the three sisters" of corn, beans, and squash. The corn provides trellises for the beans, the squash leaves discourage weeds and retard evaporation, and the beans fix nitrogen that enhances soil fertility for all three crops. Polycropping and even the planting of diverse varieties within a species also help with pest control; the different crops create more habitational niches for beneficial organisms, and harmful organisms are unlikely to have an equally devastating effect on every crop.[1]

This interrelatedness of all creatures is, in largest scope, the covenantal relationship of which García-Johnson writes that bespeaks God's unbreakable bond with the earth. We may go even further with Ramantswana who reaches beyond liberation to "reconstruction" as exemplified by Ezra and Nehemiah, who had the important work of reconstituting community in the wake of imperial devastation. We may notice that this "recovering" psalmist, in these latter verses, had energy and courage to rehabilitate his/her community after it had been devastated by the predators who almost seduced him/her.

III.

The two parts of the Psalm (vv. 2–13, 18–28) are connected by the remarkable transition in verse 17: ". . . until I went into the sanctuary of God." Already in verses 15–16 the psalmist expresses misgivings about the envy that

---

1 Davis, *Scripture, Culture, and Agriculture,* 103–4. We may also note in passing that Monica Gagliano Shechet, "A Spokeswoman for Plants that Talk") allows for plant life to be a part of the dialogue of creation.

he/she had felt toward the powerful. But now, beyond envy, the psalmist is brought up short by a temple encounter. We are not told in this terse report what happened to the psalmist in the temple. But clearly the psalmist had an encounter with the holy God who was present in invisible ways ("a voice, no form"; see Deut 4:12), whether through a declaration of the neighborly mandates of the Torah, or through the playful imagery of the liturgy, or through freighted silence that called the psalmist beyond self. Whatever happened, the psalmist is radically confronted, summoned away from the seductions of power and money, and opened to the reality and adequacy of God beyond any imagined self-sufficiency. The encounter sharply contradicted the offer of the predators in verses 2–14. In the language of García-Johnson, this is an "epistemic crisis" that is "myth-busting" in its force.[2] The "epistemic normality" of the predators is deeply subverted; there is a recognition that the proud claims of the powerful have no staying power, cannot keep their promises, and cannot make a community safe or happy. In the ancient world of the psalmist this "epistemic normality" likely was performed in the royal pageant of wealth and power. In the world of these essays the same "epistemic normality" refers to colonial modernity that legitimates land seizure and the reduction of vulnerable peasants to servitude. This instance of awareness, for García-Johnson, amounts to nothing less than the reappropriation of Christian theology. For Ramantswana it is the emergence of Black consciousness that had been severely eroded by the seeming legitimacy of apartheid. For Raheb it is the new consciousness of Palestinians that may evoke public courage. In the US church where I live, it may be a break from the dominant force of commodity consumerism, the claim of exceptionalism that issues in white nationalism, and the reliance on military power to possess the earth.

This epistemic crisis evoked for the psalmist by encounter with the holy God reduces the seduction of verses 2–14 to a readily dismissed mirage. That crisis now in the US church may summon to dig deeper into the ideological claims of US identity that has become a warrant for domination of the earth. Such work in the US church is indeed hazardous because almost all of us in the US church, most especially white Christians, are deeply inured to the taken-for-granted world of privilege.

The dramatic movement of the Psalm—*seduction* (vv. 2–14), *encounter* (v. 17) and *recovery* (vv. 18–26)—is sandwiched at the beginning and the end by clarity. The premise of the psalm is that it matters to be "pure

2. On the work of "myth-busting" in the US, see Hughes, *Myths America Lives By*.

in heart" (v. 1). It is promised by Jesus that "the pure in heart will see God" (Matt 5:8). Likely the antithesis of "pure in heart" is not an evil heart but a divided heart. The seductions of verse 2–14 depend on a divide heart, one that can never see God. Now the psalmist knows better. At the end the psalmist reflects on what has been learned through this hard journey (vv. 27–28). It has been learned that the "far from God" will come to a sorry end (v. 27). It has been learned that the "near to God" will know goodness (v. 28). The psalmist had been almost talked out of "nearness to God" by what he/she took to be a compelling alternative route to wellbeing. But now the psalmist knows better, knows through the epistemic crisis in the temple. The trust-filled affirmations of verses 18–26 fly in the face of the dominant ideology that had effectively disposed of God. In the ancient world they flew in the face of the royal-temple ideology with its land-hunger. Now they fly in the face of colonial modernity.

These strong essays will continue to echo the remarkable outcome of that epistemic crisis. When the protocols of the predators dominate, we are left in our self-sufficiency, some of us in pride, some of us in despair. But this psalm attests to *otherwise* in the ancient world of empires and peasants. And now these essays attest in our present context to *otherwise*. We may be grateful to these bold scholar-witnesses for their articulation. We may be grateful, moreover, to K. K. Yeo and Gene L. Green for organizing the conference and editing this book. It will be a durable witness as we live toward that epistemic crisis that our faith both funds and requires. We cannot force or invent that epistemic crisis upon which our future depends. We can, however, make ourselves available for such a crisis. That is what the psalmist did: make self available: "Until I went to the sanctuary of God"!

October 31, 2019 Reformation Day

Bibliography

Davis, Ellen. *Scripture, Culture, and Agriculture. An Agrarian Reading of the Bible.* Cambridge: Cambridge University Press, 2008

Hughes, Richard T. *Myths America Lives By: White Supremacy and the Stories that Give Us Meaning.* Urbana: University of Illinois Press, 2003.

Shechet, Ellie. "A Spokeswoman for Plants that Talk." *New York Times*, Style, August 29, 2019, D1–2. https://www.nytimes.com/2019/08/26/style/can-plants-talk.html.

1

The Bible and Land Colonization

Mitri Raheb

Abstract

In this chapter, I will look at one major aspect of theology of the land that is neglected, namely the colonization of land as part of colonial history and how the Bible was weaponized to legitimize such colonization. This use can be documented in several contexts such as North America, South Africa, and Australia. However, I concentrate my paper on the Palestinian context. The paper will look at the different approaches of land theologies that emerged especially in the last three decades with an emphasis on newer post-colonial approaches that advocate for the liberation of native people and their lands. I conclude with the reading of two biblical texts, one from the Old and one from the New Testament, to illustrate a Palestinian Christian theology of the land.

Introduction

On December 23, 2016, the UN Security Council met to discuss the expansion of Israeli settlement on Palestinian land in the West Bank and East Jerusalem. Resolution 2334 (2016) was adopted by fourteen countries in favor with a US (Obama Administration) abstention. The resolution reaffirmed the Security Council's stance that Israeli settlements have no legal validity and constitute a flagrant violation of the international law. The text reads as follows:

> The Security Council,
>
> "Reaffirming *its relevant resolutions . . .*
>
> "Guided *by the purposes and principles of the Charter of the United Nations, and reaffirming,* inter alia, *the inadmissibility of the acquisition of territory by force,*
>
> "Reaffirming *the obligation of Israel, the occupying Power, to abide scrupulously by its legal obligations and responsibilities under the Fourth Geneva Convention relative to the Protection of Civilian Persons in Time of War, of 12 August 1949, and* recalling *the advisory opinion rendered on 9 July 2004 by the International Court of Justice,*
>
> "Condemning *all measures aimed at altering the demographic composition, character and status of the Palestinian Territory occupied since 1967, including East Jerusalem, including,* inter alia, *the construction and expansion of settlements, transfer of Israeli settlers, confiscation of land, demolition of homes and displacement of Palestinian civilians, in violation of international humanitarian law and relevant resolutions,*
>
> "Expressing *grave concern that continuing Israeli settlement activities are dangerously imperiling the viability of the two-State solution based on the 1967 lines.*"[1]

I was watching the debate live and listened to the fourteen council members talking about the fourth Geneva Convention and international law and how important it is to abide by them. The US representative explained the decision to abstain rather than veto the resolution by saying that settlements are undermining Israel's security and eroding the prospect for a two states solution, thus the peace and stability in the area. Once all fifteen Security Council members were given the floor, it was time for Danny Danon, the Israeli representative to the UN, to address the council. This is what he said:

> Mr. President, today is a bad day for this council . . . This council wasted valuable time and efforts condemning the democratic state

---

1. "U.N. Security Council Resolution 2334 on Israeli Settlements in the West Bank and East Jerusalem."

of Israel for building homes in the historic homeland for the Jewish people. We have presented the truth time and again for this
council and implore you not to believe the lies presented in this
resolution. I ask each and every member of this council who voted
for this resolution: Who gave you the right to issue such a decree
denying our eternal rights in Jerusalem? . . . We overcame those
decrees during the time of the Maccabees and we will overcome
this evil decree today. We have full confidence in the justice of
our cause and in the righteousness of our path. We will continue
to be a democratic state based on the rule of law and full civil and
human rights for all our citizens and we will continue to be a Jewish state, proudly reclaiming the land of our forefathers, where the
Maccabees fought their oppressors and King David ruled from
Jerusalem.[2]

And just before ending his speech, something happened that captured my
full attention. Mr. Danon pulled out a Hebrew Bible, lifted it up, and said:
"This holy-book, the Bible, contains 3,000 years of history of the Jewish
people in the Land of Israel. Absolutely no one can change this history."[3]

This is the contemporary context of the land of Palestine. The biblical
story is used as history in support of a settler colonial project. Certain biblical figures are evoked to give legitimacy to an exclusivist ideology of modern
state structure. The Bible is used today by the current Israeli government, by
the Zionist movement, and by Christian Zionists to colonize Palestine and
to push its indigenous people, slowly but surely, out of the country. Beside
the Christian Zionists, there are also plenty of liberal theologians who keep
producing theological literature that provides, consciously or subconsciously, ideological cover for the colonization of Palestine.

The Context

In 1947 the Jewish population of Palestine owned about 5 percent of the
land. In the war of 1948, Israel took over 77 percent of historic Palestine,
pushed over 750,000 Palestinians out of their land, and declared their
property and a total of 86 percent as state land to be managed and used
exclusively for Israeli Jews. The Palestinians were left with 6 percent of the
land inside the Greenline. In 1967 Israel occupied the West Bank and the
Gaza Strip in addition to the Golan Heights and the Sinai. In the West

2. United Nations, Security Council, 7853rd meeting.
3. United Nations, Security Council, 7853rd meeting.

Bank, a process of land colonization has been going on since 1967 with over half of the West Bank under exclusively Israeli military control. Israel has also been investing heavily in building and subsidizing Israeli colonies, transferring over 800,000 Jewish settlers into the Palestinian territory and thus altering the demography of the West Bank. The Sinai was returned to Egypt in 1982 following the peace treaty with Egypt. Jewish settlers were evacuated from Gaza in 2005 without Israel giving up its control of the strip. In 2019 President Trump declared the Syrian Golan Heights Israeli territory and the Jewish settlements legal. Today the whole of Palestine looks like a piece of a Swiss cheese, where Israel gets the cheese, i.e. the land and the resources, while the Arab Palestinian population are pushed in the holes, overcrowded towns with no resources.

My family has its roots in Bethlehem. I was born in Bethlehem, like Jesus. In the last fifty years, Jewish settlers have been busy strangling our town with Israeli colonies. There are twenty-two of them on Bethlehem land occupied in 1967. Today the little town of Bethlehem is surrounded on three sides by a 25-foot-high wall. The wall is built in the backyard of the last home in town so that our city cannot expand. Eighty-six percent of the land of the Bethlehem governate is under Israeli exclusive control, exercised either by the Israeli colonies or by the Israeli military. There is no land left for the native people of Bethlehem and the surrounding villages to start new neighborhoods. There is not much room left within the city's boundaries for my daughters to build a home. The question about land is therefore a twofold existential question: As Palestinians, we witness on a daily basis how our land is being colonized by Jewish Israeli settlers, while as Christians, we see how the Bible, which is part of our heritage, is being used to drive such a colonial project and to render it theologically grounded.

The Bible has been used repeatedly as a justification of this land-grab and colonization. This situation is not unique to Palestine. The use of the Bible as a tool for colonization has been practiced since the sixteenth century. The land promise was used repeatedly as the pretext for land confiscation and colonization in North America, Africa, and Australia, to name a few (compare García-Johnson and Ramantswana's essays). In all cases the indigenous population was robbed of its land and livelihood, slaughtered, expelled, and the survivors confined to small territories called reservations, Bantustans, or Area A. While might was used in all cases to constitute right, the Bible was utilized to legitimize conquest and

11

colonization. In all cases the Indigenous population was demonized while the colonization was glorified as bringing light and civilization to the savage. Israel is no exception to this and must be seen within this context of European colonization. When we talk today about land theology, we cannot ignore this European history of colonization. We cannot shy away from this reception history of the Bible. And we must ask if and how to link the biblical story to history, both ancient and modern.

When Christian theologians write about Palestine, their minds are occupied with the Bible and a western-dominant narrative. They write about the land as if it exists in a vacuum; they strip it from its socio-political context, from its real people, and they rarely think about how such a theology has been and is being used to enhance settler colonialism. These occupied minds reinforce the continuing occupation of Palestine. Here I am not talking about evangelical theologians or Christian Zionists alone, but those who are well-regarded, mainline, and accomplished theologians of many denominations. In the last seventy years, many theological concepts were developed and occupied the minds of several generations of theologians worldwide. Many of these concepts might have been well intended at some point, but they mean something totally different in the current context of occupied Palestine. Theologians in their naiveté are still using a language and ideology that support current Israeli settler colonialism. Yet, we witness the emergence of new theological literature that is critical of such a reception history and of weaponizing the Bible for colonial projects.

The Literature

The colonization of ancient Canaan by the Israelites was a topic that sparked a discussion among theologians and archaeologists in the first half of the twentieth century. At the center of the debate stood the book of Joshua. Three theories were developed in this era. The American school of biblical archaeology, represented by William Albright and John Bright, defended the conquest theory by stating that the conquest under Joshua was real. The German school of Albrecht Alt and Martin Noth on the other hand, advocated the peaceful infiltration theory, meaning that the Israelites were nomads from outside who infiltrated Palestine and settled there peacefully. A third school, represented by George Mendenhall and Norman Gottwald, argued for a peasant-revolt model, saying that the Israelites were Canaanite peasants who revolted against the existing socio-political and economic structures of their time and retreated to the Highlands to form a new society.

While these debates were mainly theological in nature and eager to understand the ancient texts, these same ancient texts were weaponized and utilized as political tools by Zionist archeologists, many of whom were military generals. It is not a surprise that these archeologists were meeting in the house of Israel's first prime minister, Ben-Gurion, where "the book of Joshua was the most popular in these lively debates, and Joshua son of Nun was the star of the show."[4] Joshua must have been a role model for these Jewish Zionist military generals in the 1948 war, and they might have found the book to be a blueprint for the ethnic cleansing of Palestine.

The interest in the issue of land got new wind in Christian circles after the establishment of the State of Israel in 1948. One of the first theological reactions came from Holland. Already in 1949 the General Synod of the Dutch Reformed Church[5] adopted "the dialogue with Israel" as the calling of the church. In the new church confession document adopted in 1959, the church used the Zionist idea of the unity of people and land for the Jews, and went even further to describe the State of Israel as the "Sign of God's faithfulness."[6] These two elements, "unity of God, land and people," and a "theological attribute to the State of Israel" became important features of Protestant liberal theologies of the seventies and eighties. We find these concepts in different shades used by theologians like Hendrikus Berkhof[7] in Holland; Helmut Gollwitzer,[8] Friedrich Wilhelm Marquardt,[9] Rolf Rendtorff,[10] Peter von der Osten-Sacken[11] and Bernhard Klappert[12] in Germany; and Paul van Buren,[13] Franklin Littell,[14] Roy Eckardt,[15] and

4. Sand, *The Invention of the Jewish People*, 109.

5. It was this same church that used the Bible in a similar way to colonize South Africa and to legitimize the apartheid system. For more, see the essay by Ramantswana in this volume.

6. Kickel, *Das gelobte Land*, 158–66.

7. Drost, *A Century of Interplay*, 49.

8. Kickel, *Das gelobte Land*, 186–90.

9. Marquardt, *Die Bedeutung der Landverheissügen fuer die Christen*.

10. Kickel, *Das gelobte Land*, 194–202.

11. Kickel, *Das gelobte Land*, 194–202.

12. Kickel, *Das gelobte Land*, 194–202.

13. Haynes, "Christian Holocaust Theology," 553–85.

14. Haynes, "Christian Holocaust Theology," 553–85.

15. Haynes, "Christian Holocaust Theology," 553–85.

W. D. Davies[16] in the US. On the Catholic side there were people like the French Philosopher Jacques Maritain,[17] and theologians like Kurt Hruby, Clemens Thoma,[18] and Franz Mussner.[19] Almost all of these theologians were influenced one way or another by the Christian Holocaust theology and are considered as liberal Christian Zionists who attempted to resurrect liberal Protestant support for Israel.[20] One important characteristic of this genre of theology was that the native people of the land (the Palestinians) were not visible at all. They have been totally erased as if the land was kept unpopulated *terra nullius*. There were only a few theologians in this era who saw an issue here that needed to be addressed. Markus Barth wrote a book in 1975 titled *Der Jude Jesus, Israel und die Palaestinenser*,[21] and Rosemary Ruether,[22] who used to belong to the Holocaust theologians in the seventies, underwent a change of approach in the eighties.

Beside the Christian Holocaust theologians, there were other Biblical and Old Testament theologians who were writing on the issue of land without necessarily connecting it to the State of Israel. In 1977, the well-known American Old Testament scholar, Walter Brueggemann, published his book titled *The Land*. In this book, Brueggemann responded to an emerging American context where many people felt a "sense of being lost, displaced, and homeless."[23] This existential and socio-psychological yearning for a secured place led Brueggemann to claim that the land is the "central theme in biblical faith"[24] and is primarily concerned "with the issue of being displaced and yearning for a place."[25] In this book, Brueggemann talks about three important aspects of the land. He speaks of the land as a gift, a temptation, and a task, thus emphasizing the dialectic between landlessness and landedness.[26] Norman Habel, a Lutheran Australian Old Testament scholar published a book in 1995 titled *The Land Is*

16. Davies, *The Territorial Dimension of Judaism*.

17. Kickel, *Das gelobte Land*, 134–36.

18. Kickel, *Das gelobte Land*, 141–45.

19. Kickel, *Das gelobte Land*, 146–47.

20. Haynes, *Christian Holocaust Theology*.

21. Barth, *Der Jude Jesus, Israel und die Palästinenser*.

22. Ruether, *The Wrath of Jonah*.

23. Brueggemann, *The Land*, 1.

24. Brueggemann, *The Land*, 3.

25. Brueggemann, *The Land*, 2.

26. Brueggemann, *The Land*, xi.

Mine: Six Biblical Land Ideologies. As the title implies, Habel was already aware that land theology is always an ideology "which employ[s] theological doctrines, traditions, or symbols to justify and promote the social, economic and political interests of a group within society."[27]

All these different writings about the land took place in a context of Jewish religious nationalism and "messianism," when extremist Jewish groups within Israel started settling in the West Bank claiming it as ancient "Judea and Samaria." "Judea and Samaria" was not so much a geographical description as a religious claim with a political agenda. A process of "Judeaization" of the country was taking place, where settlers would build Jewish settlements on every tel that had a biblical connection. Israeli archeologists were digging in the West Bank, Jerusalem, and the Haram as-Sherif in particular. Many of them, like Moshe Dayan and Yohanan Aharoni, were advocating a greater Israel after the "Kingdom of David."[28]

In December 1987 the first Intifada, or Palestinian Uprising, broke out. The pictures of Israeli tanks on one side and Palestinian kids on the other were screened on TV worldwide. The Intifada gave Palestinian people in general and Palestinian Christians in particular the courage to tell their stories. In response to this changing context, new theological movements evolved in Palestine concentrated around three important centers in the Bethlehem and Jerusalem area.[29] These church-related centers in Palestine became more vocal and involved in communicating the untold story of the Palestinian people in the land of Palestine, resulting in creating more awareness at the ecumenical level by making mainstream Christian Churches more alert to the situation in Palestine.

27. Habel, *The Land Is Mine*, 10.

28. Sand, *The Invention of the Jewish People*, 112–15.

29. Al-Liqa' Center established the conference of "Theology and the Local Church in the Holy Land." This conference was established in 1987 for the purpose of formulating a local theology and for forming a literary, renaissance, and religious movement to contribute to the creation of an ecumenical movement in Palestine. This conference brought forth the "Basic Document on Theology and the Local Church." The second center was Sabeel. Sabeel Center for Liberation Theology was established in 1989 by Naim Ateek. "Sabeel is an ecumenical grassroots liberation theology movement among Palestinian Christians. Inspired by the life and teaching of Jesus Christ, this liberation theology seeks to deepen the faith of Palestinian Christians, promote unity among them, and lead them to social action." And finally, Dar Annadwa Addawliyyah was established in 1995 by Mitri Raheb with the aim of "equipping the local community to assume a proactive role in shaping their future." Developing a Christian theology for the Palestinian context, supporting the emergence of contextual Palestinian Christian art and music, and organizing international theological encounters soon became three distinct activities for Dar Annadwa.

This period was characterized by the abundance of Palestinian theological publications by theologians coming from diverse backgrounds, such as: Elias Chacour,[30] Jiries Khoury,[31] Michel Sabbah,[32] Mitri Raheb,[33] Munib Younan,[34] Naim Ateek,[35] Odeh Rantisi,[36] Rafiq Khoury,[37] Riah Abu Asal,[38] and others.

Once the Palestinians started to raise their voices and tell their story, the world could no longer ignore them. By the early 1990s the initial responses to their cries showed the shortcomings and misuse of biblical scholarship in relation to the land and the Palestinian people.

The first and most important writing on this subject hailed from a British scholar, Keith Whitelam, as early as 1991 under the title, *The Invention of Ancient Israel: The Silencing of Palestinian History.*[39] Whitelam argued that ancient Israel was invented and created after the image of the European nation-state, thus retroacting the modern state of Israel into the Iron Age. In this context, Thomas Thompson[40] and the Copenhagen School[41] triggered the so-called minimalist debate questioning the biblical historiography of "ancient Israel" because it confuses the biblical story with actual evidence-based history.

Other responses came from postcolonial biblical scholars, most of them living like the Palestinians on the margin. Robert Allen Warrior,[42]

30. Chacour, *Blood Brothers*; Chacour, *We Belong to the Land.*

31. Khoury, *The Uprising on Earth* [in Arabic]; Khoury, *Arab Christians* [in Arabic]; Khoury, *Arab Christians and Muslims* [in Arabic].

32. Sabbah, *Reading the Bible in the Land of the Bible.*

33. Raheb, *I Am a Palestinian Christian*; Raheb, *Bethlehem Besieged*; Raheb, *Faith in the Face of Empire*; Invention of History (Conference) Bethlehem, *The Invention of History*; Raheb, *The Biblical Text in the Context of Occupation.*

34. Younan, *Witnessing for Peace*; Younan, *Our Shared Witness.*

35 Ateek, *Justice, and Only Justice*; Ateek, *A Palestinian Christian Cry for Reconciliation*; Ateek, Duaybis, and Tobin, *Challenging Christian Zionism*; Ateek, Ellis, and Ruether, *Faith and the Intifada*; Ateek et al., *Holy Land, Hollow Jubilee.*

36. Rantisi, *Blessed Are the Peacemakers.*

37. Khoury, *The Card of the Compatriot* [in Arabic]; Khoury, *Palaestinensisches Christentum*; Khoury, *Editorials for the Time to Come* [in Arabic].

38. Abu El-Assal, *Caught in Between.*

39. Whitelam, *The Invention of Ancient Israel.*

40 Thompson, *Early History of the Israelite People.*

41. Lemche, *Ancient Israel*; Ahlstrom and Rollefson, *The History of Ancient Palestine*; Davies, *In Search of "Ancient Israel."*

42. Warrior, "A North American Perspective," 289.

himself a Native American, read the biblical story through the eyes of the Canaanites. The Chinese theologian Pui-Ian Kwok struggled with the question: "Can I believe in a God who killed the Canaanites and who seems not to have listened to the cry of the Palestinians now for some forty years?"[43] In 1997, Michael Prior investigated and showed clearly "how the biblical account has been used to justify the conquest of land in different regions and at different periods, focusing on the Spanish and Portuguese colonization and settlement of Latin America, the white settlement in southern Africa, and the Zionist conquest and settlement in Palestine."[44]

Jewish theological voices too started to be heard critiquing the policies of the State of Israel, Marc Ellis[45] perhaps the most vocal among them. During the Oslo Process the interest in the issue of land was weakened, maybe because people thought that peace was coming and the land would ultimately be shared among Israeli and Palestinians. But with the second Intifada, the interest in the issue of land was renewed. Biblical theologians were no longer able to ignore the Israeli/Palestinian conflict.

In the preface of the second edition[46] of his book on the land, Brueggemann discussed five major developments in Old Testament studies that needed to be taken into account in 2002 at the height of the second Intifada that were not on his radar at the time of his initial scholarship in 1979. One of them was:

> the recognition that the claim of 'promised land' in the Old Testament is not an innocent theological claim but is a vigorous ideological assertion on an important political scale. This insight is a subset of ideology critique in the field that has emerged as a major enterprise only in the last decades. Perhaps the most important articulation in this matter is the recognition of Jon Levenson that Israel's tradition demonizes and dismisses the Canaanites as a parallel to the anti-Semitism that is intrinsic to the New Testament. That is, Israel's text proceeds on the basis of the primal promises of Genesis 12–36 to assume entitlement to the land without regard to any other inhabitants including those who may have been there prior to Israel's emergence . . . The shortcoming in my book reflects my inadequate understanding at that time, but also reflects

43. Kwok, *Discovering the Bible in the Non-Biblical World*, 99.

44. Prior, *The Bible and Colonialism*, 11.

45. Ellis, *Israel and Palestine out of the Ashes*; Ellis, *Toward a Jewish Theology of Liberation*; Ellis, *Judaism Does Not Equal Israel*.

46. Brueggemann, *The Land*.

the status of most Old Testament studies at that time that were still innocently credulous about the theological importance of the land tradition in the Old Testament . . . Most recently scholarly attention has been given to the ongoing ideological force (and cost) of the claim of 'promised land'. On the one hand, this ideology of land entitlement . . . has served the ongoing territorial ambitions of the state of Israel, ambitions that, as I write (April 2002), are enacted in unrestrained violence against the Palestinian population.[47]

What Brueggemann did was unveil the national Israeli agenda behind the religious packaging. The native peoples of the land—the Canaanites and the Palestinians—were identified by Brueggemann by name and the suffering inflicted on them under religious pretext was finally highlighted. Unfortunately, Brueggemann failed to continue along this path in his latest book *Chosen?: Reading the Bible amid the Israeli-Palestinian Conflict*. In fact, in *Chosen?* Brueggemann's writing is very similar to the writing of liberal Christian Zionists.

In the aftermath of the second Intifada we see a renewed attempt by mainline Palestinian Christian theologians, like Paul Tarazi,[48] and others to write about the land.

However, it is interesting that many of the theologians writing about the land in the last two decades came from the evangelical spectrum. Gary Burge,[49] Stephen Sizer,[50] Peter Walker, and Philip Johnston from the Anglo-Saxon world, and Salim Munayer,[51] Yohanna Katanacho,[52] and Munther Isaac[53] from Palestine. In most of these writings one finds several attempts at producing a biblical theology that does not shy away from confronting it with the current political reality, though the answer is not always convincing. Returning to the universalization of the land promise, or saying that the promise is fulfilled in Jesus, or that the land belongs to God, does not address the political claim by Israel. Yet, these writings are important attempts to reach out to the evangelical community as a means of a kind of damage control. All these writings have a reconciliatory attitude—calling

---

47. Brueggemann, *The Land*, xiii–xiv.

48. Tarazi, *Land and Covenant*.

49. Burge, *The Bible and the Land*; Burge, *Whose Land?*; Burge, *Jesus and the Land*.

50. Sizer, *Christian Zionism*.

51. Munayer and Loden, *The Land Cries Out*.

52. Katanacho, *The Land of Christ*.

53. Isaac, *From Land to Lands*.

for a sharing of the land. However, this conclusion comes often disconnected from the biblical theological discourse.

An interesting development that coincided with the second Intifada but was a result of the Iraq War, was the emergence of imperial studies. Theologically, this led theologians to focus on the study of the Roman Empire. Richard A. Horsley,[54] Warren Carter,[55] and others began looking at the Old and New Testaments in relation to the empire. Although most of these studies were done by biblical scholars, many of them were applying what they learned about the Roman Empire to the American Empire. They would talk about biblical Israel facing different empires, but they failed to make a direct connection from there to the modern Middle East, connecting the empire with the modern State of Israel, and the Palestinians with biblical Israel. Norman Gottwald in his article, "Early Israel as an Anti-Imperial Community" paints a highly idealistic picture of ancient Israel. But then concludes:

> To complete the analogy, the present-day equivalent of ancient Israel might properly be relatively powerless countries like Cuba, Nicaragua, Chile, Venezuela, Vietnam, and Iraq, all of whom have been the object of hostility and aggression from the American Empire. And in a supreme irony, Palestinians of the West Bank may most nearly approximate the early Israelites since they occupy the same terrain, practice similar livelihoods, and long for deliverance from the 'Canaanite' State of Israel backed by the American Empire.[56]

In recent years, several scholars like Luis Rivera Pagan,[57] Fernando Segovia,[58] Mitri Raheb,[59] Santiago Slabodsky,[60] and others have begun to write about certain aspects of the land issue using a decolonial, post-colonial, or cultural critical approaches. Steven Salaita did a groundbreaking comparative analysis of Native American and Palestinian literature showing

---

54. Horsley, *Jesus and the Politics of Roman Palestine*; Horsley, *In the Shadow of Empire*; Horsley, *Paul and the Roman Imperial Order*; Horsley, *Jesus and the Powers*.

55. Carter, *Matthew and Empire*; Carter, *The Roman Empire and the New Testament*.

56. Gottwald, "Early Israel as an Anti-Imperial Community," 24.

57. Rivera-Pagan, "Toward an Emancipatory Palestinian Theology," 89–118.

58. Segovia, "Engaging the Palestinian Theological-Critical Project," 29–80.

59. Raheb, *Faith in the Face of Empire*.

60. Slabodsky, *Decolonial Judaism*.

how settler colonial societies weaponize biblical stories as national histories to justify their colonial projects.[61]

One interesting development in recent years was the post-national work of the Oslo group on Jesus and cultural complexity.[62] In his essay on the present debate of the historical Jesus, James G. Crossley situates the discussion of the Jewish Jesus within the political context after the 1967 war between Israel and the neighboring Arab states. Crossley sees that war as a major turning point towards a very pro-Israel political attitude in the US, UK, and other European countries, and he finds that this attitude strongly influences scholarly perspectives in Jesus Studies. The implicit presuppositions of most historical Jesus Studies, he argues, are pro-Israel, and anti-Arab and Palestinian. Crossley shows clearly "how New Testament and Christian origins scholarship is profoundly influenced by and supportive of contemporary Anglo-American power."[63] This thesis was investigated further by Halvor Moxnes in *Jesus and the Rise of Nationalism: A New Quest for the Nineteenth-Century Historical Jesus,* where Moxnes shows how the rise of nationalism in Europe and the beginnings of the historical Jesus studies in the nineteenth century identified Jesus and Christianity "with national identities and with Western colonialism and imperialism."[64] Land theologies were among the casualties of such colonial Christianity.

Maybe for this reason Norman Habel had to go back to Abraham in his discussion of the same topic. In his booklet *Acknowledgement of the Land and Faith of Aboriginal Custodians after following the Abraham Trail,*[65] published in 2018, Habel recognized that most of the land

61. Salaita, *Holy Land in Transit*; Salaita, *Inter/Nationalism.*

62. Moxnes et al., eds., *Jesus beyond Nationalism*; West and Crossley, eds., *History, Politics and the Bible.*

63. Moxnes et al., eds., *Jesus beyond Nationalism*, 195.

64. Moxnes et al., eds., *Jesus and the Rise of Nationalism*, 1.

65. Habel, *Acknowledgement of the Land.* "I have written this book in response to an invitation of my mentors, The Rainbow Spirit Elders, who wrote, 'Abraham, the peacemaker, respected the peoples of the land. We ask the same. Abraham recognised the God of the land. We ask the same. Abraham and the peoples of the land shared mutual blessings. We ask the same'" (*Rainbow Spirit Theology* 1997, p. 85)." On the back cover of his book, Norman Habel writes, "My goal in this book is to follow the Abraham trail through the legends of Genesis and beyond so as to retrieve, where possible, how Abraham related to the indigenous Canaanites, their God and their land. What I believe I have retrieved provides a precedent for settlers who have dispossessed the land and discounted the faith of the Aboriginal Peoples where they settled. In the light of the Abraham precedent and subsequent colonial history, it is time to go beyond making another apology and make a

theologies are utilized by colonizers and are never concerned with the perspective of the colonized. Habel learned through an Aboriginal elder, George Rosendale, to read the land theology from the perspective of the colonized. He quotes George saying:

> Little was said (by the missionaries) about the indigenous people of the land whom the Israelites conquered. No questions were asked about whether Joshua's scorched Earth policy was what God really wanted for the indigenous people. Today Joshua's mode of operation sounds to us very much like that of the British colonial conquerors. Did the British have to follow Joshua's way?[66]

This perspective of the colonized people helps Habel to acknowledge "that the classical promised land ideology seems to reflect a bias based on a belief that one chosen people has a divine mandate to invade and possess a particular land and dispossess the indigenous inhabitants of that land as peoples without rights, peoples such as the Australian Aboriginal Peoples."[67]

Habel concludes his booklet by urging the church and its theologians to grasp the Kairos moment, follow the model of Abraham thus changing their theology, attitude, and practice. He writes:

> Yes!
>
> IT IS TIME!
>
> In the light of the faith of Abraham,
>
> the positive relationships between Abraham
>
> and the indigenous custodians of Canaan,
>
> including worship of El, the Creator Spirit of Canaan,
>
> a covenant with the same Canaanite God,
>
> a treaty in which this God, Abraham, the Canaanites
>
> and the land of Canaan are partners,
>
> AND
>
> In the light of how Australian settlers, influenced by a promised land ideology,
>
> Dispossessed the indigenous custodians,
>
> Discounted their creation spirituality

---

formal acknowledgement that leads to a genuine treaty process."

66. Habel, *Acknowledgement of the Land*, 12.

67. Habel, *Acknowledgement of the Land*, 42.

And violated the land they held sacred.

IT IS TIME

For Christian Churches

And the descendances of Christian settlers

To follow the precedent of Abraham,

To make a public acknowledgment,

A colonial confession,

AND

To promote a treaty process

That guarantees and respects the identity, rights,

Sovereignty, country and spirituality

Of the Aboriginal Peoples.[68]

Last but not least, in 2014 The Palestine History and Heritage Project (PaHH) was launched with theologians from the Copenhagen School as well as Palestinian and Israeli scholars with the aim of producing a trustworthy history of Palestine, "which may reflect Palestine's multi-vocal and multi-faceted history in a form that is scholarly evidence based rather than rooted in traditional religious interpretation."[69] A first volume of this work came out in 2019 under the title *A New Critical Approach to the History of Palestine*,[70] following Nur Masalha's book on *Palestine: A Four Thousand Year History*,[71] showing the uninterrupted use of the name Palestine from the time of Ramses III until today. This corresponded well with Shlomo Sand's book on the *Invention of the Land of Israel* in 2012,[72] where Sand illustrated how the concept of a Jewish homeland was invented by Evangelical Christians together with Jewish Zionists to facilitate the colonization of Palestine. Sand stands in continuity with Whitelam; what the latter tried to show for Old Testament scholarship, Sand illuminates as part of racial and political nineteenth-century European history.

68. Habel, *Acknowledgement of the Land*, 74.

69. Hjelm, "The Palestine History and Heritage Project (PaHH)," 9.

70. Hjelm et al., *A New Critical Approach to the History of Palestine*.

71. Masalha, *Palestine*.

72. Sand, *The Invention of the Land of Israel*.

The Power of Naming Things

Part of the colonization project is re-naming the colonized land. This is done to erase the indigenous history of the land and the identity of its native people. After conquering Carthage, the Romans coined the word "Africa" to refer to that conquered region, which later was expanded as a name for the whole continent. Spanish conquerors renamed Anahuac to become America.[73] Naming is thus a way to exercise power and to claim dominion over land and people. By evoking a biblical name "Israel" for a modern state in 1948, the Jewish immigrants wanted to instrumentalize a certain aspect of the ancient biblical story for the creation of a new exclusive national identity while at the same time erasing the name Palestine and thus marginalizing its indigenous people.

There are many reasons why I opted in this paper to call the land between the Mediterranean and the Jordan river Palestine rather the Israel. Historically speaking, the name Israel referred mainly to the northern part of land, during a relatively short period of time, known as the Kingdom of Israel or House of Omri (tenth century to 720 BCE). This region, called later Samaria, was interestingly enough a "non-Jewish" section of the land. This entity must be distinguished from biblical Israel as a theological concept. Both in turn are different than "Ancient Israel" as a modern construct that confuses certain aspects of the biblical story with history, thus projecting an exclusive ethno-national and religious state into the Bible, which is then used by the current Israeli government as a pretext for land colonization.[74] It is almost certain that the term "Land of Israel" took root in rabbinic Judaism only after the destruction of the Temple. No wonder that the term is found only one time in the entire Bible, in Matt 2:21. However,

> the Christian or rabbinic incarnation of the term is not identical in meaning to the term as employed in the context of Jewish connection to the territory in the age of nationalism . . . Only in the early twentieth century, after years in the Protestant melting pot, was the theological concept of 'Land of Israel' finally converted and refined into a clearly geonational concept. Settlement Zionism borrowed the term from rabbinic tradition in part to displace the term 'Palestine,' which . . . was then widely used not only throughout Europe but also by all the first-generation Zionist leaders. In

73. For more, see the paper of García-Johnson in this volume.

74. More on these three different uses of the word "Israel" by Davies, *In Search of "Ancient Israel."*

the new language of the settlers, the Land of Israel became the exclusive name of the region.[75]

In this paper I have chosen to relate to the land as the land of Palestine,

> Because it is the most consistent name of the area stretching from as far north as Sidon to the Brook of Egypt and from the Mediterranean into the Transjordan with ever changing borders since the Iron Age. It is testified in inscriptions from Ramses III (ca. 1182–1151) with increased regional comprehension in the 12th–10th century BCE. From the neo-Assyrian period (tenth to seventh century BCE) onwards it is the most common etic collective designation, manifested in the Roman period (first century BCE to fourth century CE).[76]

While the Assyrians already under Ramses III have used the name in the form of *Pilishtu* to describe the coastal region of the land, it was the Greek historiographer and cartographer, Herodotus (ca. 484–425 BCE), who re-crafted the term to become *Palaistine*, referring to the entire land including even Transjordan.[77] There is, in fact, no other name for this land that has been continuously in use for almost 2,500 years and until today other than Palestine. So why abandon it? Why replace it? Why adopt a settler colonial appropriation of a biblical name? In addition, it is only this name that historically had an inclusive character. Palestine in this sense does not refer to a political or ethnic entity, but rather to a multi-ethnic, multicultural and multi-religious region that was able to include diverse identities and peoples within its boundary. So why adopt an exclusive term that manifest itself today in an Israeli state that is meant exclusively for its Jewish immigrants over and against the native people whose roots have been in the land for millennia?

In the context of land colonization, theologians have to be very careful not to supply the colonizer with the ideological tools that supports their oppression. As Jasper asked,

> What can hermeneutics, as we have been studying it, contribute to the *ethical* dilemmas posed when texts of power become texts of terror? Can we stand neutral, as merely 'academic interpreters? Is hermeneutics necessarily a political activity? We need to be aware that such a pernicious political program as apartheid in South

75. Sand, *The Invention of the Land of Israel*, 28.

76. Hjelm, "The Palestine History and Heritage Project (PaHH)," 11.

77. Masalha, *Palestine*, 72–73.

Africa had its beginnings in particular biblical hermeneutics that saw all things created as distinct under God, their differences to be clearly acknowledged.[78]

. . . .

We might also recall that apartheid in South Africa arose, to some extent at least, from biblical criticism and interpretation. In the postcolonial era of the present day it is easy to see how a very difficult hermeneutic pertains, and how not only is the Bible to be read in a different way in the light of political and social experience, but the power of the new reader must be turned against old prejudices that were once regarded as unquestioned truths.[79]

We cannot separate Israeli colonial policies in Palestine from the modern European colonial history. No credible theologian today would accept a land theology from the whites in South Africa, or North America, or Australia. Why would they accept it from Israel? Why is Israel's colonization of Palestine seen as unique, biblical, and different from all others? We cannot be so theologically naïve as to talk about "the land," meaning Palestine, without reflecting on the current usage of land ideology by Jewish colonial settlers. No one should be allowed, not Jewish settlers, nor Israeli politicians, nor naïve Christian theologians, to use "biblical rights" to violate "human rights." We should not allow for accusations of anti-Semitism and the western guilt of the Holocaust to avert our eyes from Israel's colonial policies. It might be that the missionaries to the Americas in the sixteenth century were innocent, and it might be that Brueggemann in the late seventies was naïve, but it is high time to end this theological innocence. We ought to confess that Christian theologians have been playing, consciously or subconsciously, a major role in aiding the ongoing colonization of Palestinian land and people. The land theology was one of the theological tools used for Palestinian dispossession and oppression. Therefore, there is a dire need for a de-colonial theology of the land.

Towards a De-colonial Theology of the Land

An important element of the land that has not been given enough attention is the geo-politics. When it comes to geo-politics, one must examine the context of the land and its native people. These two elements, land

78. Jasper, *A Short Introduction to Hermeneutics*, 122–24.

79. Jasper, *A Short Introduction to Hermeneutics*, 125.

and people, are the most important hermeneutical keys to understanding Scripture and interpreting it.

The Geo-Politics and the Land

Historic Palestine is a land located at the crossroads of three continents and is anything but isolated. Palestine as a land has the image of being the heart of the region, the "navel of the earth," and the center of the universe. However, this is myth. In reality, Palestine is a land on the margin, on the periphery of the Fertile Crescent, a borderland for diverse empires. A close look at the map will show Palestine surrounded by five regional powers who determined its fate: Egypt to the south, Europe to the west, Turkey to the north and Mesopotamia and Persia to the northeast. Throughout history, Palestine has stood in the sphere of influence of one or two of these five powers, which pulled it in competing directions. Palestine's fertile plains have been battleground for these conflicting powers, and it is hardly by chance that Armageddon is seen as taking place in the land's most fruitful valley.

Due to its geo-political position, Palestine has been occupied by or under the patronage of Egyptians, Assyrians, Babylonians, Persians, Greeks, Ptolemies, Seleucids, Romans, Byzantines, Arabs, Crusaders, Ottomans, British, and Israelis. While these superpowers were well-established politically, having accumulated a culture of political dominance, the native peoples of Palestine were powerless most of the time, constantly adjusting their identity and boundaries within a changing context. In fact, adjustment, resistance, and liberation from occupation is a connecting thread of Palestine's history from the second millennium BCE until today.

The land often came under more than one imperial power, fostering diverse identities. The influence of regional powers over Palestine created either a buffer zone or a battlefield, where regional wars were fought. None could truly survive if it were not supported by its greater patrons serving their interests. If one looks at these features of Palestine, one would see how the geo-politics of the region practically determine the land's fate, a fate that is very difficult to escape. Being a land under occupation, the theme of liberation was central throughout history as well as in the Bible. At the same time, control of the land and the unity of its peoples remains an uphill struggle.

The Native People and the Land

Many Christian theologians and Zionist thinkers confuse the Israelites of the Bible with the Israelis of today. They shift between 70 CE and 1948 as if history stood still for two millennia and as if the land of Palestine were "without a people," waiting to be inhabited "again" by "a people without a land." Behind such an understanding is a static view of history and a fundamentalist approach to biblical literature.

Most of Palestine's native people never left. Only a small minority of Palestine's people suffered deportation. Empires came, occupied the land for a number of years or decades, but they were eventually forced to leave again. The majority of the native people remained in the land of their forefathers and foremothers. They were the 'am ha-'aretz, the "people of the land," in spite of all the empires that have controlled that land throughout its history. Identities, however, kept changing in accord with new realities and empires. People changed their language from Palestinian and Phoenician West Semitic to Aramaic and Hebrew and later to Greek and Arabic. Their identity shifted from Canaanite, Philistine to Judahite and Israelite, to Hasmonean, to Roman, to Byzantine, to Arab, to Ottoman and Palestinian, just to name a few. They changed religion from Ba'al to Yahweh. Later they believed in Jesus as the Christ and became Christians, who were first Aramaic-speaking monophysites, before being forced to become, for example, Greek Orthodox. Obligated to pay extra taxes during Islamic dominance, they became Muslims. And yet, throughout the centuries, they maintained a dynamic and flexible identity. In this sense, Palestinians of today stand in historic continuity with biblical Canaanites, Philistines, Israelites, and Judahites. Just so are the Palestinians the native people of the land. The Palestinian people (Muslims, Christians, Jews, and Samaritans) with a significant continuity from biblical times until the present are the native people who survived empires and occupations. They are also the remnant of invading armies or settlers who stayed in the land and integrated themselves rather than returning to their original homeland. Palestinians are the outcome of this long and dynamic history. Their context is important for understanding the Bible. It is time to listen to the narrative of the native people of the land.

The Palestinians of today are the native people of the land because they are not part of the empire. Their voice is not only unheard, but often silenced. Unless their discourse falls within a European framework, they are not considered dialogue partners. The Muslims of Palestine are ignored because they are Muslims and not thought of as part of the Judeo-Christian culture. Palestinian Christians are marginalized because they are Palestinians. And native, anti-Zionist Jews and Samaritans, who are neither Zionist nor Ashkenazi, are ignored as non-European. Many western theologians want to monopolize the discourse, allowing only those Palestinians who use their frame of reference.

If we really want to understand the Bible's message, it is of the utmost importance to listen to Palestine's native people. Their suffering under occupation, their aspiration for liberation, their struggles and hopes are all relevant to exegesis. For the Palestinian people land is life. It is ancestral heritage. They belong to this land and have no where else to go. They experience, however, how they are made aliens at home by Israeli politics. They see how Jewish immigrants can occupy their land, build settlements, get citizenship, while they, the native people, are marginalized and pushed out. Palestine is their homeland, and yet those Palestinians in the diaspora are not allowed to enter the land of their fathers while Jews irrespective where they live are given the right to settle anywhere in Palestine. The Land of Palestine is colonized by the military and by the Bible. The natural right of the Palestinians to the land of their ancestors is violated. This is not an exclusive Palestine experience, but it is the experience of many of the native peoples in North and South America, in Southern Africa and Australia. The voice of these indigenous peoples is important to listen to. The Bible is the book that contains these voices, the voices of the colonized not the colonizers.

Reading Scriptures through Palestinian Eyes

Allow me here to share my reading as a Palestinian Christian theologian of two scriptural passages, one from the Old Testament and one from the New:

1 Kings 21

Ahab, king of Samaria, had a palace in Jezreel. But Ahab was not satisfied with his large palace. He coveted the vineyard of his neighbor Naboth. Ahab wanted Naboth's vineyard at any price. First, he offered him a "better one." But he was also ready to pay him with silver. In vain. Naboth did not want to give away his ancestral inheritance. To keep his inheritance was something like divine command to Naboth. But Ahab also knew that as king of Israel he had no right to confiscate the land of an Israelite farmer. In accordance with Israelite faith, even the Israelite kings were subject to divine law. But Jezebel, the Sidonian king's daughter, had a different belief and thus a different understanding of royalty. That is why she asked her husband whether he was really still king of Israel when he did nothing about Naboth's refusal. Jezebel's models were the imperial rulers, who were absolute sovereigns. It was the occupier–occupied relationship, where the law serves the empire and its policy of expansion.

So, Jezebel asked for two scoundrels to bear false witness against Naboth, saying: "You have cursed God and the king." The divinity of God and security of the state represented by the king were of utmost importance. Naboth was stoned to death, and Ahab was then free to confiscate all his possessions. In this context, the prophet Elijah intervened because injustice was committed, God's commandments were violated, and the court was misused.

The story of Naboth is the story of thousands of Palestinians today whose lands are confiscated to enlarge the Jewish colonies in the West Bank that are exploiting the water and resources of the Palestinian people. Naboth's story is taking place almost on a daily basis in the West Bank. It is a clear violation of the divine law and a clear violation of international law, and yet there are only very few theologians who dare to raise a prophetic voice calling this land colonization by name.

Mathew 5:5

One of the sentences of Jesus that requires re-interpretation is Mathew 5:5, "Blessed are the meek for they will inherit the Earth." This text is taken from the Sermon on the Mount according to Matthew. Compared with the other beatitudes of that sermon, this one is often neglected and seldom receives attention. The phrase: "Blessed are the peacemakers," is cited frequently, but we rarely hear "Blessed are the meek for they will inherit the Earth." Indeed, Luke doesn't even mention this verse but skips it altogether. Interestingly, Luke likes to talk about the poor, the hungry, and the thirsty, but not about the meek!

This verse must have been largely ignored initially because it was translated incorrectly. Originally the verse was taken from Psalm 37, which doesn't talk about "the Earth," but "the land." In fact, "the land" is repeated several times in that psalm. It should, therefore, read, "Blessed are the meek; they will inherit the land." That perhaps makes better sense. Psalm 37 does not talk about the land near and far but does speak about a certain land, Palestine. When Jesus said that the meek will inherit the land, everyone at the time knew what was meant by the land. He meant the Holy Land, Palestine. When the words of Jesus were translated from Aramaic into Greek the word that means the land was changed to read the Earth. In fact, in Arabic the word *alard* means both "earth" and "land." Translation is interpretation. Earth replaced land.

The Gospels were closely connected to a certain land, Palestine. For the early Church, located outside of Palestine, talking about the Earth made far more sense. Why should somebody in Rome worry about who would inherit Palestine? They were concerned about their souls and maybe about their own land, but not about a distant one. Yet one cannot understand the gospels if they are disconnected from their original context, which is Palestine.

I struggled with this text for many, many years. It simply did not make sense. I do not like to spiritualize things because I think Jesus always spoke to reality, refusing to avoid it, which was the essence of his spirituality. For a long time I thought that Jesus had been mistaken. One needs only to look around the West Bank to realize who controls the land. Sixty percent of the West Bank is controlled by the Israeli army and Jewish settlers. This glaring reality is one of the largest land thefts in modern history, worth hundreds of billions of dollars. If one looks at the Israeli settlements, which ring the West Bank, it is all too obvious that the empire has inherited the land. Listening to the words of Jesus, through Palestinian, Native North American, Black South African, or Aboriginal Australian ears, therefore, does not offer much help; it does not make more sense of Jesus' words. He must have been mistaken! It is all too obvious that the military occupation controls the land, and that it also controls that land's resources. Everything is controlled by the empire. The empire inherits the land, not the meek. Jesus was mistaken because the meek are crushed. Their land is being confiscated to make place for people brought in by the empire. Jesus was mistaken.

But in the last decade, while struggling with this text, I have come to read it with new eyes. In the process I discovered something more powerful than I expected. Mathew 5:5 actually speaks directly to reality in a way we would never imagine. It is necessary to use *longue durée* lenses, because if the verse is read with regular lenses, we will never grasp its true meaning. Our mistake has been to read history only with the current empire in mind. The prevailing empire takes all our attention. This is the problem if people look at the Israeli-Palestinian conflict only from a perspective of the last seventy years. If we look solely at the last seven decades, the word of Jesus doesn't make sense at all. But Jesus had wide-angle lenses and he looked at history *longue durée*. For the people in Jesus' day, the occupation began with the Romans. Jesus had a far greater understanding of the history of Palestine. He looked at a thousand years all at once and he saw a chain of empires. There is not a single regional empire that at some point did not occupy Palestine. The first empire to occupy Palestine was the Assyrian in 722 BC who came and stayed for over two hundred years. They were replaced by the Babylonians in 587, who didn't last because they were pushed out by the Persians in 538. The latter didn't stay long either because they were forced to leave by Alexander the Great. Then there were the Romans. Two thousand years after Jesus we can continue reciting the list of empires who ruled Palestine: the Byzantines, the Arabs, the Crusaders, the Ayyubids, the Ottomans, the British, and last, but not least, the State of Israel. We have been trained to naively connect Israel today with the Israel of the Bible, instead of connecting it to the above chain of occupying empires. If we focus on the latter, Jesus' words make perfect sense. None of those empires lasted in Palestine forever. They came and stayed for fifty, one hundred, two hundred, a maximum four hundred years and in the end, they were all blown away, gone with the wind.

When occupied people face the empire, they generally become so overwhelmed by its power that they start to think that the empire will remain forever and has eternal power. Jesus wanted to tell his people that the empire would not last, that empires come and go. When empires collapse and depart it is the poor and the meek who remain. The haves from the people of the land immigrate; they seek to grow richer within the centers of empire. Those who are well-educated are brain-drained and vacuumed up by the empire. Who remains in this land? The meek, i.e., the powerless! Empires come and go, while the meek inherit the land. Jesus' wisdom is staggering. It seems to me we have been blinded by a theology that failed to help us understand what Jesus was really saying. Some might disagree, insisting that the Israeli occupation is different. They say, "Look at the settlements. How can you claim they will be gone one day? Look at the wall. How can you say it will be dismantled?" But Israel is no different from the empires of the past. The native people of Palestine who lived at the time of Jesus and saw the military checkpoints that Herod the Great had created such as Herodian, Masada, and many others, would never have imagined that Herod and his empire were not there permanently. If one looks at the "settlements" and cities built by Herod and his sons, such as Caesarea Maritima, Caesarea Philippi, Sepphoris, Tiberias, Sebastopol, Jerusalem, and others, it would have been almost inconceivable to question the durability of the Roman empire. Jesus was telling the Palestinian Jews that the Romans who had built those settlements would not be there forever and Palestine would be inherited by the meek. Is this a cheap hope in a distant future? No. Jesus wanted to release the powerless from the power of the empire. The moment he spoke those words, the empire lost its power over the people, and power was transferred where it rightly belonged, with the people.

Conclusion

The Land issue is not a mere theological topic but one of high political relevance. Historically, the notion of the promised land was used by western Christian empires to colonize and exploit countries and continents. While no one dares today to use such a theology for colonization, the State of Israel does. In the last hundred years, Israel has been colonizing Palestinian land often under the pretext of the Bible. The Zionist movement developed to that end an ideology of "God, people, and land" being an inseparable unit. This ideology was adopted not only by conservative Christian Zionists but also by Christian Holocaust theologians and other Christian liberal Zionists. Such an adaptation might have been a reaction to a formal anti-judaistic theologies or out of guilt of the Holocaust, but this same theology resulted in giving Israel a theological impunity to continue to colonize Palestinian land. Such theologies contradict international law and are in violation of the charter of Human rights. Yet such theologies continue to be developed by naïve or well-intentioned theologians or others brought in by the Zionist movement. It is high time to develop a theology that takes the colonization of Palestine as part and parcel of European colonial history into consideration. It must trouble theologians when the promised land becomes the colonized land. When indigenous peoples are robbed of their land and resources and left landless or refugees or confined in reservations. In the last two decades we saw the emergence of new theological voices in Australia, Canada, and other places recognizing the lawful owners of the land; nothing like this is yet seen in Israel. It is high time that theologians listen to and amplify the indigenous voices of the people of the land rather than being an uncensored echo of imperial colonial powers. The Bible contains texts of liberation and not texts of colonization. God is the God of justice and does not tolerate oppression. The imperial British policy of divide and rule along sectarian lines created part of the problem we face today. The current Israeli government implements an ethno-nationalist policy of ethnic cleansing of the indigenous people based on an exclusive "biblical" myth-history and should not be justified theologically or politically. Palestine, throughout history, was pluralistic in nature. Until 1948 Christians, Jews, and Muslims were able to share the land and live side by side. What vision do we develop for our land: an exclusive ethnocentric vision or an inclusive one that respects the plurality of peoples and their identities? This question is of utmost importance, not only for the future of Palestine, but for the entire world facing today's ethno-national tensions, exclusive ideologies, and religious fanaticism.

For Further Reading

Habel, Norman C. *Acknowledgement of the Land and Faith of Aboriginal Custodians after Following the Abraham Trail*. Eugene, OR: Wipf & Stock, 2018.
Hjelm, Ingrid, Hamdan Taha, Ilan Pappe, and Thomas L. Thompson, eds. *A New Critical Approach to the History of Palestine*. Palestine History and Heritage Project 1. New York: Routledge, 2019.
Liew, Tat-siong Benny. *Colonialism and the Bible: Contemporary Reflections from the Global South*. Postcolonial and Decolonial Studies in Religion and Theology. Lanham, MD: Lexington, 2018.
Raheb, Mitri. *Faith in the Face of Empire: The Bible through Palestinian Eyes*. Maryknoll, NY: Orbis, 2014.
Salaita, Steven. *Inter/Nationalism: Decolonizing Native America and Palestine*. 3rd ed. Minneapolis: University of Minnesota Press, 2016.
Sand, Shlomo. *The Invention of the Land of Israel*. London: Verso, 2012.
West, Jim, and James G. Crossley. *History, Politics and the Bible from the Iron Age to the Media Age: Essays in Honour of Keith W. Whitelam*. Library of Hebrew Bible/Old Testament Studies 651. London: Bloomsbury T. & T. Clark, 2017.

Bibliography

Abu El-Assal, Riah. *Caught in Between: The Story of an Arab Palestinian Christian Israeli*. London: SPCK, 1999.
Ahlstrom, Gosta W., with Gary O. Rollefson. *The History of Ancient Palestine*. Edited by Diana Edelman. Minneapolis: Fortress, 1993.
Ateek, Naim Stifan. *A Palestinian Christian Cry for Reconciliation*. Maryknoll, NY: Orbis, 2008.
———. *Justice, and Only Justice: A Palestinian Theology of Liberation*. Maryknoll, NY: Orbis, 1989.

Ateek, Naim Stifan, Cedar Duaybis, and Maurine Tobin. *Challenging Christian Zionism: Theology, Politics and the Israel-Palestine Conflict.* London: Melisende, 2005.

Ateek, Naim Stifan, Marc H. Ellis, and Rosemary Radford Ruether. *Faith and the Intifada: Palestinian Christian Voices.* Markyknoll, NY: Orbis, 1992.

Ateek, Naim Stifan, Michael Prior. *Holy Land, Hollow Jubilee: God, Justice, and the Palestinians.* London: Melisende, 1999.

Barth, Markus. *Der Jude Jesus, Israel und die Palästinenser:* Zürich: TVZ-Verlag, 1975.

Brueggemann, Walter. *The Land: Place as Gift, Promise, and Challenge in Biblical Faith.* 2nd ed. Overtures to Biblical Theology. Minneapolis: Fortress, 2002.

Buck, Mary Ellen. *The Canaanites: Their History and Culture from Texts and Artifacts.* Eugene, OR: Cascade Books, 2019.

Burge, Gary M. *Jesus and the Land: The New Testament Challenge to "Holy Land" Theology.* Grand Rapids: Baker Academic, 2010.

———. *The Bible and the Land: Uncover the Ancient Culture, Discover Hidden Meanings.* Ancient Context, Ancient Faith. Grand Rapids: Zondervan, 2009.

———. *Whose Land? Whose Promise?: What Christians Are not Being Told about Israel and the Palestinians.* Cleveland: Pilgrim, 2003.

Burns, Duncan, and John W. Rogerson, eds. *Far from Minimal: Celebrating the Work and Influence of Philip R. Davies.* Edited by Duncan Burns and John W. Rogerson. Library of the Hebrew Bible/Old Testament 484. London: T. & T. Clark, 2012.

Carter, Warren. *Matthew and Empire: Initial Explorations.* Harrisburg, PA: Trinity, 2001.

———. *The Roman Empire and the New Testament: An Essential Guide.* Abingdon Essential Guides. Nashville: Abingdon, 2006.

Chacour, Elias. *Blood Brothers.* Grand Rapids: Chosen Books, 1984.

———. *We Belong to the Land: The Story of a Palestinian Israeli Who Lives for Peace and Reconciliation.* San Francisco: Harper & Row, 1992.

Davies, Philip R. *In Search of "Ancient Israel": A Study in Biblical Origins.* 2nd ed. London: T. & T. Clark, 2015.

Davies, W. D. *The Territorial Dimension of Judaism.* Berkeley: University of California, 1982.

Ellis, Marc H. *Israel and Palestine out of the Ashes: The Search for Jewish Identity in the Twenty-First Century.* Sterling, VA: Pluto, 2002.

———. *Judaism Does not Equal Israel.* New York: New Press, 2009.

———. *Toward a Jewish Theology of Liberation: The Challenge of the 21st Century.* 3rd exp. ed. Waco, TX: Baylor University, 2004.

Finkelstein, Israel. *The Quest for the Historical Israel: Archaeology and the History of Early Israel.* Atlanta: Society of Biblical Literature, 2007.

Gottwald, Norman K.. "Early Israel as an Anti-Imperial Community." In *In the Shadow of the Empire: Reclaiming the Bible as a History of Faithful Resistance,* edited by Richard A Horsley, 9–24. Louisville: Westminster John Knox, 2008.

Habel, Norman C. *Acknowledgement of the Land and Faith of Aboriginal Custodians after Following the Abraham Trail.* Eugene, OR: Wipf & Stock, 2018.

———. *The Land Is Mine: Six Biblical Land Ideologies.* Overtures to Biblical Theology. Minneapolis: Fortress, 1995.

Haynes, Stephen R. "Christian Holocaust Theology: A Critical Reassessment." *Journal of the American Academy of Religion* 62 (1994) 553–85.

Hjelm, Ingrid. "The Palestine History and Heritage Project (PaHH)." In *The Ever Elusive Past: Discussions of Palestine's History and Heritage*, 9–19. Beirut: Dar Al Nasher, 2019.

Hjelm, Ingrid, Hamdan Taha, Ilan Pappe, and Thomas L. Thompson, eds. *A New Critical Approach to the History of Palestine*. Palestine History and Heritage Project 1. New York: Routledge, 2019.

Horsley, Richard A., ed. *In the Shadow of Empire: Reclaiming the Bible as a History of Faithful Resistance*. Louisville: Westminster John Knox, 2008.

———. *Jesus and the Politics of Roman Palestine*. Columbia: University of South Carolina, 2014.

———. *Jesus and the Powers: Conflict, Covenant, and the Hope of the Poor*. Minneapolis: Fortress, 2011.

———. *Paul and the Roman Imperial Order*. Harrisburg, PA: Trinity, 2004.

Invention of History (Conference) Bethlehem, West Bank. *The Invention of History: A Century of Interplay between Theology and Politics in Palestine*. Bethlehem: Diyar, 2011.

Isaac, Munther. *From Land to Lands; from Eden to the Renewed Earth: A Christ-Centred Biblical Theology of the Promised Land*. Carlisle, UK: Langham Monographs, 2015.

Jasper, David. *A Short Introduction to Hermeneutics*. Louisville: Westminster John Knox, 2004.

Katanacho, Yohanna. *The Land of Christ: A Palestinian Cry*. Eugene, OR: Pickwick Publications, 2013.

Khoury, Jiries. *The Uprising on Earth and the Uprising in Heaven* [in Arabic]. Jerusalem: Al-Liqa' 1989.

———. *Arab Christians* [in Arabic]. Jerusalem: Al-Liqa' 2001.

———. *Arab Christians and Muslims: Past, Present and Future* [in Arabic]. Jerusalem: Al-Liqa' 2001.

Khoury, Rafiq. *The Card of the Compatriot: Afflictions and Hopes* [in Arabic]. Jerusalem: n.p., 1985.

———. *Palaestinensisches Christentum*. Berlin: Aphorisma, 1993.

———. *Editorials for the Time to Come* [in Arabic]. Jerusalem: Al-Liqa', 1996.

Kickel, Walter. *Das gelobte Land: Die religiöse Bedeutung des Staates Israel in jüdischer und christlicher Sicht*. Munich: Kösel, 1984.

Kwok, Pui-lan. *Discovering the Bible in the Non-Biblical World*. Bible & Liberation. Maryknoll, NY: Orbis, 1995.

Lemche, Niels Peter. *Ancient Israel: A New History of Israel*. 2nd ed. London: T. & T. Clark, 2015.

Liew, Tat-siong Benny. *Colonialism and the Bible: Contemporary Reflections from the Global South*. Lanham, MD: Lexington, 2018.

Marquardt, Friedrich-Wilhelm. *Die Bedeutung der Landverheissugen für die Christen*. Munich: Kaiser, 1964.

Masalha, Nur. *Palestine: A Four Thousand Year History*. London: Zed, 2018.

———. *The Bible and Zionism: Invented Traditions, Archaeology and Post-Colonialism in Palestine-Israel*. New York: Zed, 2007.

Moxnes, Halvor. *Jesus and the Rise of Nationalism: A New Quest for the Nineteenth-Century Historical Jesus*. New York: IBTaurus, 2012.

Moxnes, Halvor, Ward Blanton, and James G. Crossley, eds. *Jesus beyond Nationalism: Constructing the Historical Jesus in a Period of Cultural Complexity.* Bible World Oakville, CT: Equinox, 2009.

Munayer, Salim, and Lisa Loden. *The Land Cries Out: Theology of the Land in the Israeli–Palestinian Context.* Eugene, OR: Cascade Books, 2012.

Prior, Michael. *The Bible and Colonialism: A Moral Critique.* Biblical Seminar 48. Sheffield: Sheffield Academic, 1997.

———. *Zionism and the State of Israel: A Moral Inquiry.* New York: Routledge, 1999.

Raheb, Mitri. *Bethlehem Besieged: Stories of Hope in Times of Trouble.* Minneapolis: Fortress, 2004.

———. *Faith in the Face of Empire: The Bible through Palestinian Eyes.* Maryknoll, NY: Orbis, 2014.

———. *I Am a Palestinian Christian.* Minneapolis: Fortress, 1995.

———. *The Biblical Text in the Context of Occupation: Towards a New Hermeneutics of Liberation.* Bethlehem: Diyar, 2012.

Rantisi, Audeh G. *Blessed Are the Peacemakers: A Palestinian Christian in the Occupied West Bank.* Grand Rapids: Zondervan, 1990.

Rivera-Pagan, Luis N. "Toward an Emancipatory Palestinian Theology: Hermeneutical Paradigms and Horizons." In *The Biblical Text in the Context of Occupation: Towards a New Hermeneutics of Liberation,* edited by Mitri Raheb, 89–118. Bethlehem: Diyar, 2012.

Ruether, Rosemary Radford. *The Wrath of Jonah: The Crisis of Religious Nationalism in the Israeli–Palestinian Conflict.* San Francisco: Harper & Row, 1989.

Sabbah, Michel. *Reading the Bible in the Land of the Bible.* Jerusalem: LPJ, 1993.

Salaita, Steven. *Holy Land in Transit: Colonialism and the Quest for Canaan.* Syracuse: Syracuse University Press, 2006.

———. *Inter/Nationalism: Decolonizing Native America and Palestine.* 3rd ed. Minneapolis: University of Minnesota Press, 2016.

Sand, Shlomo. *The Invention of the Jewish People.* New York: Verso, 2009.

———. *The Invention of the Land of Israel.* New York: Verso, 2012.

Segovia, Fernando F. "Engaging the Palestinian Theological-Critical Project of Liberation: A Critical Dialogue." In *The Biblical Text in the Context of Occupation: Towards a New Hermeneutics of Liberation,* edited by Mitri Raheb, 29–80. Bethlehem: Diyar, 2012.

Sizer, Stephen. *Christian Zionism: Road Map to Armageddon?* Leicester, UK: Inter-Varsity, 2004.

Slabodsky, Santiago. *Decolonial Judaism: Triumphal Failures of Barbaric Thinking.* New York: Palgrave Macmillan, 2014.

Sugirtharajah, R. S. *Exploring Postcolonial Biblical Criticism: History, Method, Practice.* Malden, MA: Wiley-Blackwell, 2012.

Tarazi, Paul Nadim. *Land and Covenant.* Myrtle Beach, SC: OCABS Press, 2009.

Thompson, Thomas L. *Early History of the Israelite People: From the Written and Archaeological Sources.* Studies in the History of the Ancient Near East 4. Leiden: Brill, 1992.

"U.N. Security Council Resolution 2334 on Israeli Settlements in the West Bank and East Jerusalem." Submitted by Senegal, Malaysia, Venezuela and New Zealand, December 23, 2016. http://www.tedmontgomery.com/bblovrvw/Endtimes/U.N.resolution.draft.html.

United Nations, Security Council, 7853rd meeting (Friday, 23 Dec 2016, 2pm): https://unispal.un.org/DPA/DPR/unispal.nsf/9a798adbf322aff38525617b006d88d7/9097bdd8e5efe8678525809800550e37, accessed April 19, 2020.

Warrior, Robert Allen. "A North American Perspective: Canaanites, Cowboys, and Indians." In *Voices from the Margin: Interpreting the Bible in the Third World*, edited by R.S. Sugirtharajah, 287–95. London: SPCK, 1991.

West, Jim, and James G. Crossley. *History, Politics and the Bible from the Iron Age to the Media Age: Essays in Honour of Keith W. Whitelam*. Library of Hebrew Bible/Old Testament Studies 651. London: Bloomsbury T. & T. Clark, 2017.

Whitelam, Keith W. *The Invention of Ancient Israel: The Silencing of Palestinian History*. New York: Routledge, 1996.

Younan, Munib. *Our Shared Witness: A Voice for Justice and Reconciliation*. Minneapolis: Lutheran University Press, 2012.

———. *Witnessing for Peace: In Jerusalem and the World*. Minneapolis: Fortress, 2003.

2

Faith Seeking for Land

A Theology of the Landless

Oscar García-Johnson

Abstract

The chapter identifies the necessary processes to disarticulate a colonizing theological cartography that for five centuries has operated transforming global colonial powers into *landlords* and conquered peoples into *landless* of the world. The chapter also identifies the necessary elements to articulate an indigenous theology of the land-less that I call Trans-Americanity. Informed by theology, biblical interpretation, and decoloniality, Trans-Americanity offers a new epistemic transformation that uncovers the dignity of the lands and peoples of the Americas in a way that makes possible the Zapatista dictum: "a world in which many worlds fit."

Introduction

Theresa Yugar writes a letter,

Dearest Eva (Life),
I write this letter to ask your forgiveness
for my complicity in the denigration of our natural world . . .
We have forgotten who we are . . . our Story . . .

there were no inequalities, or hierarchies, between humans and nonhumans.

Humans were called to be good stewards of all creation.

Earth was a gift to us. Humans chose to exploit the gift,

rather than to understand it and share it . . .

Western ideologies have stripped religious symbols of the sacred . . .

in God's name [they] have distorted their sacred Scriptures.

We need to remember that Earth is a living organism

who preserves our past, sustains our present, and promises our future.

To kill Her is to kill us.

Responsibility to Her echoes our responsibility to God.[1]

The cartographic and political imagination of the west that led to the conquest of the Americas and the subsequent colonial acts have been deeply theological, as I show in the first part of this chapter. The social imaginary of Europeans was transformed when they discovered the route across the Atlantic and came to experience the vastness and diversity of the lands and peoples of *Anáhuac* (regions of Mesoamerica), *Tahuantinsuyu* (regions of South America), and *Ayiti* (regions of the Caribbean).

For a handful of western powers, the epistemic transformations that took place in the sixteenth century through the so-called "discovery of the New World" prompted a new way to imagine themselves and relate to the world. Local European kings and kingdoms became global landlords. And local indigenous kingdoms and civilizations became a global labor force and landless peoples. These transformations inform the theologies of the land developed in the context of the Americas. What we call today's global migration crisis, which includes forced migration, exile, massive deportation, and so on, is more accurately a five-hundred-year problem spawned by global designs built with great political and economic imagination and legitimized by westernizing theologies of the land.

A decolonial theological framing that I call Transoccidentality undergirds this new cartographic imagination. Over the course of various colonial acts since the first day of the European conquest, a contesting Transoccidental imaginary has operated both epistemically and ethically in certain sectors of the Americas. This Transoccidental imaginary has built epistemic

1. Yugar, "Letter to Eva," 341–42.

resistance in an attempt to construe alternative worlds at the border of the invented colonial/modern geography we now call America. What I call *faith seeking for land* is an epistemic "homing device"[2] that represents a decolonial search for Trans-Americanity—the *traditioning* of Pachamama[3] and human dignity (*humanitas*)—both crucial values lost in the colonial creations of the conquest, colonization, and western modernization in the American Global South (Latin America and its diaspora).

The Day before America Became Someone's Land

The story of the theology of the American land can be traced to the fifteenth century, and more precisely to May 3, 1493. It was on that day that Pope Alexander VI, a native of Valencia in Spain, issued a papal bull titled *Inter Caetera* (or Bulls of Donations), by which he assigned the Spanish and Portuguese crowns spatial, political, and juridical privileges on territories known and to become known in the future of the West Indies and Africa. *Inter Caetera* informed the Treaty of Tordesillas (1494), and this in turn can serve us today as a case study for the origination of premodern international laws.

May 2, 1493, can be claimed as the last day on which the Original American territories of *Anáhuac* (regions of Mesoamerica), *Tahuantinsuyu* (regions of South America), and *Ayiti* (regions of the Caribbean) did not yet exist or have a name in the cartographic imagination of the European powers of the fifteenth century—the day before America became somebody's land or property. A brief quotation from this document gives us an idea of the extent of the geopolitical privileges given to the Iberian powers in the fifteenth to seventeenth centuries:

> Among other works well pleasing to the Divine Majesty and cherished of our heart, this assuredly ranks highest, that in our times especially the Catholic faith and the Christian religion be exalted and be everywhere increased and spread, that the health of souls be cared for and that barbarous nations be overthrown and brought to the faith itself . . . [W]e . . . assign to you and your

2. See Hidalgo, *Revelation in Aztlán*.

3. *Pachamama* was (and still is) honored as Mother Earth by the Andean indigenous populations. The return to ancestral wisdom in the critical thinking of the Americas has recovered the significance of Pachamama in the current ecological discourse of the Global South.

40

heirs and successors, kings of Castile and Leon, . . . all islands and mainlands found and to be found, discovered and to be discovered towards the west and south, by drawing and establishing a line from . . . the north, . . . to . . . the south, . . . the said line to be distant one hundred leagues towards the west and south from any of the islands commonly known as the Azores and Cape Verde.[4]

This papal bull, along with other treaties that followed, instrumentalized the right of Iberian powers to explore and occupy non-European spaces that they deemed to be "uncivilized, half-civilized, leaderless, and empty."[5] Immediately after the European discovery of the Atlantic passage, a number of European legal theologians began to debate the legitimacy of the conquest and the extent to which the church might rightfully support the establishment of the colonial order in the West Indies. However, the dominant tone of the debate revolved not around the *undoing* of the conquest—as if the Iberian powers would simply withdraw from occupied territories. (This was indeed an aspiration of some Indigenous intellectuals in the sixteenth century, among them Guamán Poma de Ayala.) Rather, the debates sought to provide a moral-theological basis on which to come to terms with the idea of occupying the land and justifying slavery as a viable economic system while evangelizing the "uncivilized." A brief account of the arguments suffices to convey the necessary background.

On the one hand, we see legal theologians like John Mair (Scotland) and Juan Ginés de Sepulveda (Spain) claiming that Spain had the "divinely ordained right" to take possession of the new-found lands and exploit both the lands and its inhabitants—on the basis of the Europeans' perception of the Indigenous Peoples as non-Christian, savages, barbarians, and cannibals.[6] On the other hand, we see a combination of Indigenous rights activist-theologians like Antonio de Montesinos[7] and Friar Bartolomé de las Casas and legal theologians like Francisco de Vitoria condemning "the

---

4. Pope Alexander VI, "Inter Caetera."

5. See Smichtt, *The Nomos of the Earth*, 11.

6. Medina, *Christianity, Empire and the Spirit*, 108, 127.

7. The "Requerimiento," from which we get this language of "divinely ordained right" was drafted in response to Montesinos's public rebuke of the colonial effort to degrade American Indigenous Peoples. Montesinos's sermon asked a set of poignant questions: "By what right, with what justice, do you hold these Indians in such cruel and horrible servitude?" The Requerimiento sought to legitimize the colonial atrocities by building its "theology" over the foundation of biblical texts such as Deut 20:10–12. See Koschorke et al., eds., *A History of Christianity in Asia, Africa, and Latin America, 1450–1990*, 286–89.

colonizing measures of the Spaniards as immoral" and even questioning the legitimacy of the conquest on the basis of the natural right of Indigenous Peoples to the titles of their lands.[8] Clearly this idea of "titles of the land" reflects the western imagination, not that of the Peoples of *Anáhuac*, *Tahuantinsuyu*, and *Ayiti* for whom Mother Earth could not be owned. European arguments in favor of the Peoples' natural rights to the titles of the land were rhetorical rather than rational because the Europeans questioned the very essence and quality of Indians' humanity (*humanitas*). Las Casas acknowledged that the human inferiority (on the basis of their alleged barbarism) of the People of the Americas was a stigmatized notion in the public imagination of his contemporaries and fueled an ambitious epistemic project: that of showing that barbarism ought not to be understood as the basis of human inferiority, for many European kingdoms and civilizations were themselves barbaric. But his project largely failed during his lifetime, although he did gain legal concessions in favor of American Indigenous communities.[9]

The predicament for western Christianity in this historical venture was that *Inter Caetera* not only gave Iberian powers the rights over territories and peoples but also commission a "religious mission" to those people and lands, or so argue some colonial critics.[10] This bifocal divine commission essentially endorsed Europeans' inauguration of a western "system of cultural otherization" that continues to this day through a series of colonizing/modernizing acts.[11]

The Christian Cartographic Imagination of the West and the Invention of America

Inter Caetera (the Bull of Donations) along with other conquest documents shaped and validated the self-projection of Europeans as administrators of God's earth on the basis of a skewed theological imaginary. This theological imaginary justified the European conquest, colonial order, and the creation of the modern states. How this theological imaginary came to be in the first place, and how it came to the point of endowing a church office (that of Pope Alexander VI) with the power to issue a "legal" document that gave

8. Medina, *Christianity, Empire, and the Spirit*, 125, 127.

9. See Brunstetter and Zartner, "Just War against Barbarians," 733–52.

10. See Valdeón, *Translation and the Spanish Empire in the Americas*, 109–10.

11. Medina, *Christianity, Empire, and the Spirit*, 127.

"international" power to European crowns over massive portions of lands and countless populations of the non-European world is something that requires attention in our discussion of a theology of the land, or better still, a theology of the land-lords and land-less.

In an attempt to develop an African Christology from a Postcolonial perspective, theologians Victor I. Ezigbo (Nigerian) and Reggie L. Williams (African American), undertake an interesting theological project that can inform our critical inquiry. They begin their deconstructive Christological work by engaging with Walter Mignolo, a noted de/postcolonial theoretician from Argentina. In itself, this interdisciplinary (South-to-South) engagement is a game changer for theology. Ezigbo and Williams argue that the "colonial distortion of Christianity" emerged from cultural imperialism, which transpired from the uneven relationship between Europeans and non-Europeans across the centuries.

Ezigbo and Williams's appropriation of Mignolo's critical views to frame theologically how colonial modernity invented the white imperialist Christ is important for our American context because it suggests how we might use decolonial theories to rebuild theological perspectives non-Eurocentrically. In Ezigbo and Williams's engagement with Mignolo's work *The Idea of Latin America,* what stands out are the epistemic mechanisms by which the white imperialist Christ and a number of other fictional populations and geographies (savages, barbarians, the uncivilized, The West Indies, The New World, Latin America, The Orient, etc.) come to life as creations of colonial modernity. The following points are noteworthy:

1. By the fifteenth century, there was a popular cartographic-theological understanding of the world as being divided into three parts—Africa, Europe, and Asia—thanks to Augustine of Hippo (*City of God*) and some early Christian biblical traditions.

2. Spanish cartographers of the time adopted the understanding that the three parts of the world corresponded to the three sons of Noah: Japheth (Europe), Ham (Africa), and Shem (Asia).[12]

3. Ethno-racial categories were building up in the theological imaginary of pre-modern Europe before they were embedded into culture, economics, and politics

---

12. Mignolo's most complete discussion on the pre-and-post-Hispanic cartographic imaginations can be found in Mignolo, *The Darker Side of the Renaissance,* chap. 5 and 6.

a. By portraying Japheth as a collective people destined to "expand into non-European lands, subjugate the inhabitants and assimilate them into European Christian imagination";[13]

b. By promulgating the curse-of-Ham narrative in "which people of color—typically of African descent—are destined to be subjugated (by Japheth)";[14] and

c. By naturalizing the geopolitics of race and ethnicity in colonial territories after the sixteenth century (Mignolo), and advancing the idea of supersessionism (Europe self-imagined as the New Chosen People of God) that had been established since early Christian times and had come to occupy a place within colonial/modern categories.

4. "The Christian narrative of racially-divided continents" participated in the creation of an "imperialist (white) Christ" who, in turn, legitimized the subjugation of Africans, Original Americans, and non-Europeans in general. "Europe became a process that created people, inventing them . . . as savages."[15]

In many ways, my work follows a similar trajectory to that of Ezgbo and Williams.[16] I concur that westernized Christology is a problem in the development of colonial modernity. I also concur that we should use decolonial theories to map the genealogy of race and ethnicity, epistemic hierarchies, power differentials, and global designs. That the making of world theological scholarship requires shifting away from Euromerican-centrism

13. Ezigbo and Williams, "Converting a Colonialist Christ," 89.

14. Ezigbo and Williams, "Converting a Colonialist Christ," 90.

15. Ezigbo and Williams, "Converting a Colonialist Christ," 91. Clearly this premodern biblical reading is misleading both in terms of context and textual logic. The contextual translation is guided by a cartographic imagination based on hyper-local imperial hierarchies aligned with the spirit of the time (Iberian grandiosity). In terms of following the logic of biblical texts such as Gen 9:20–27, one finds no way to justify the idea of total domination by Japheth. The offspring of Ham (supposedly Africa) were to be servants of Shem (supposedly Asia). However, Japheth's (supposedly Europe) blessing does not entitle him to subjugate Shem (supposedly Asia) and Ham's (supposedly Africa) offspring: "may Canaan be the slave of Japheth" (v. 27). Japheth does not live in Shem's tent as an overlord. Both share the same authority over Ham's children. So, Japheth, if we were to follow literally the divine blessing, is to share authority with Shem. In the flow of literal textual meaning, Shem is not servant to Japheth. This type of biblical interpretation fails to do justice to the text and its context, on all counts.

16. See García-Johnson, *Spirit Outside the Gate,* chap. 7.

is another parallel that the three of us share. But there are important differences as well. I move beyond Ezigbo and Williams regarding the assumptions that 1) coloniality has distorted Christian theology, and that 2) we can or ought to "convert" distorted theological constructions like the "colonialist Christ." On the former, I affirm (with other decolonial thinkers like Mignolo himself) that normative Christian theology in the West is implicated in the construction of both the logic of coloniality and the rhetoric of modernity. Coloniality has been theologized just as much as theology has been colonized. Hence an expression of Christian theology *per se* is not something we see affected by an external force, vis-à-vis coloniality. It is internal. In short, there is no colonial modernity without westernizing Christian theology. The so-called "Christological distortion" is part of the epistemic and ethical self-positioning of Christianity as a western phenomenon, which in turn has built coloniality and modernity since the sixteenth century. On the latter, I will continue to argue that "the Christological imagination of the Americas has been wounded by the experiences of the conquest and colonial rule" to the point of requiring an exit and rerouting by means of a decolonial pneumatological turn.[17] Both elements endemic to European colonization—colonial wound and Christology—are intricately related to the corporeal disembodiment of land (Pachamama) and human dignity (*humanitas*) in the peoples and lands of the Americas. Thus, a reconceived theology of the land would require a re-origination on the basis of a decolonial pneumatology. This will be my final point. But I begin with colonial Christology and its implications for the development of the theologies of the land in the Americas.

The Making of a Theology of the *Land-lords* and the *Land-less*

The European theological cartographies that led to the conquest and subsequent colonialities in the Americas found concrete expression in the fictional construction of *another land*. In the case of the Americas, this land came to be invented in a series of geopolitical acts: The West Indies, The New World, America (continent), Latin America, and *America* (the US national narrative). The theology of the land in the Americas begins with the narrative of invented lands and peoples in a series of successive epistemic acts. In Walter Mignolo's words: "America was not an existing entity to be

17. García-Johnson, *Spirit Outside the Gate*, 104.

discovered. It was invented, mapped, appropriated, and exploited under the banner of the Christian mission."[18]

Here, "Christian mission" is not to be confused with "universal Christianity"—as if such a reality ever existed historically beyond the rhetoric of Christendom and cultural imperialism.[19] Christianity has always been experienced, developed, and transmitted as a local expression of embodied faith. To say it with the Roman Catholic systematic theologian Orlando Espín: "Christians believe a Christianity that is what they believe Christianity is . . . Christianity does not exist and has never existed as a living religion apart from Christians."[20] Or as I say it with Dyrness in *Theology Without Borders*: "theology develops in a particular place out of the interaction . . . between some version of the Christian tradition and the indigenous traditions of that place—both cultural and religious."[21]

In sum, the Christianity that developed in the Iberian Peninsula and was transmitted through the conquest and subsequent colonial acts was local, hegemonic, and counter-reformational, and became globalizing for a period through the process of the conquest and colonial rule. This expression of Christianity energized a world system that developed over time. It is responsible for today's global designs only due to "the magnitude of the transformation of multiple worlds that began in the sixteenth century" as

18. Mignolo, *The Darker Side of Western Modernity*, 6. During the Renaissance and the Enlightenment, coloniality emerged as a new structure of power as Europeans colonized the Americas and built on the ideas of Western civilization and modernity as the endpoints of historical time and Europe as the center of the world. Walter D. Mignolo argues that coloniality is the darker side of Western modernity, a complex matrix of power that has been created and controlled by Western men and institutions from the Renaissance, when it was driven by Christian theology, through the late twentieth century and the dictates of neoliberalism. This cycle of coloniality is coming to an end. Two main forces are challenging Western leadership in the early twenty-first century. One of these, "dewesternization," is an irreversible shift to the East in struggles over knowledge, economics, and politics. The second force is "decoloniality." Mignolo explains that decoloniality requires delinking from the colonial matrix of power underlying Western modernity to imagine and build global futures in which human beings and the natural world are no longer exploited in the relentless quest for wealth accumulation.

19. Even when the early Mignolo can be charged with exercising the essentialism that he critiques when applied to Christian missions or Christianity, his situated critique of western universalized local histories and more recent acknowledgment of the internal counternarratives produced by border (non-hegemonic) christianities must be taken into account when using his approaches. In other words, with proper criticism Mignolo's research can be very useful and goes beyond Mignolo's own ideological preferences.

20. Espin, *Idol and Grace*, xxiii.

21. Dyrness and García-Johnson, *Theology without Borders*, 43.

the "Atlantic connected European initiatives, enslaved Africans, [and] dismantled [indigenous] civilizations."[22] How did the matrix of colonial power launch the production of *landlords* and the *landless* in the Americas that would define American theology of the land for generations?

The theological cartography that oriented the project of the conquest and the various colonial acts that have taken place since the sixteenth century operated fundamentally as an epistemic and ethical machine. As I elaborate in *Spirit Outside the Gate*:

> Nature as an experiential reality took a different meaning for the originating cultures: it became detached from the human experience of personal existence, a counternarrative to Pachamama, Mother Earth, which for the Aymaras and Quechuas, in contrast to the West, had no significant distinction from culture and was (still is) experienced as a unifying force of existence. A second epistemic transformation that took place, with economic and social consequences, is that Indians and Africans [and anyone from the modern Latin America later on], as Boff notes, became a dispensable labor force: fuel in a production process.[23]

We have here a conquering ethics fueled by an othering epistemic machine that transforms Mother Earth (Pachamama) and ancient civilizations (enslaved Africans and Original Americans) into exploitable land, a labor force, and soteriological objects of European Christendom. Consequently, through multiple epistemic transformational acts that happened since the sixteenth century in the Americas we see local European kings and kingdoms being transformed into global landlords and local indigenous kingdoms and civilizations being transformed into a global labor force and landless peoples.

Theological cartographies are powerful tools for justifying acquisition practices by those in control of both maps and canons. For instance, the book of Joshua 13–22 is a vivid example of "theological cartography." These are the chapters that recount the "conquered land" (conquest in this biblical context means "invaded and occupied" not fully appropriated and dominated) being divided and reorganized. What makes my argument fit with these chapters of the book of Joshua is that because the people in the land that was invaded were not displaced or annihilated, the cult of the God of the Israelites adopted elements from Canaanite religion (Judg

22. García-Johnson, *Spirit Outside the Gate*, 110.

23. García-Johnson, *Spirit Outside the Gate*, 110.

1:19–36; 2:11–13). This became a major reason for the Hebrew Bible to register God's constant rebuke of his people and its eventual demise (Isa 2:6–9; Jer 7:28–34; 17:1–4; Hos 4:11–19). As Mitri Raheb reminds us, the Hebrew Bible has frequently been used to overwrite any non-Jewish law of the land. In the same breath, empires require to be made into divine agents in order to succeed. Echoing Raheb's criticism, when we allow for ideological movements (such as Zionism) to build theologies by assembling "God, people, and land" as one inseparable unit, then "everything is controlled by the Empire. [Yet, it is not t]he empire, [but] the meek, who inherit the land"[24] of Jesus's gospel, argues Raheb. In such a predicament, empire acts like God. American, African, Asian, and Palestinian lands, for instance, were transformed into "divine property" (that is, imperial property) along with their inhabitants. In the process, sterilization or cleansing of the land has been a regulating tool for empires to gain control, which is why empires lose grip of their subjugated lands and peoples when religious blending (or so-called syncretism) is allowed. Christendom's evangelization has been strictly *antibiotical* in the sense that the so-called "native elements" of an individual or culture or community have been considered bad bacteria in need of being removed. This interpretation is well illustrated through the work of the Puerto Rican sociologist Ramón Grosfoguel and his articulation of the four great genocides/epistemicides of the western epistemic machine in the sixteenth century: 1) against the Jewish and Muslim population in the conquest of Al-Andalus, 2) against Indigenous Peoples in the conquest of the Americas, 3) against the Africans kidnapped and enslaved in the Americas, and 4) against women accused of witchcraft who were burned alive in Europe.[25]

Surprisingly, despite the costs, religious blending has survived, embedded in living religions across the world. And Indigenous communities around the world are today reclaiming their lost histories and land-based identities. But the problem is that many find themselves land-less. Knowing how these transformations into landlords and the landless took place helps us to appreciate how different Indigenous communities are re-appropriating their identities through their lands and ancestral memories.

My inquiry into colonial Christology has revealed how these transformations took specific shape in the making of *landlords* and *landless*

24. Raheb, *Faith in the Face of Empire*, 91. See also his essay in this volume.

25. See Grosfoguel, "The Structure of Knowledge in Westernized Universities."

populations in the Americas. Here, I offer only a brief summary of the theology of the land-lord and land-less based on colonial Christology.[26]

In colonial critical history, we see how every major project of western evangelization of the Americas, whether of Roman Catholicism or western Protestantism, built colonizing/modernizing layers into the social imaginary of the so-called agents of salvation (Euromerican missions) and the objects of evangelization (Latin Americans and their global diaspora). The work of Leonardo Boff and Walter Mignolo is helpful in outlining four corresponding epistemic invasions to illustrate how the theology of the land-lord and land-less was built and sustained across the centuries.[27] (A fifth one emerged after 2001. This I discuss separately in the next section on Trans-Americanity.) We can think of these four invasions as epistemic-geopolitical building blocks instrumentalized by a rhetoric of salvation and carrying implications on the control of lands and peoples in the American Global South.

1. Salvation by Colonial Economy and Civilizing Christianization (1500s–1800s)

This first invasion was foundational, determinative, and open-ended, and consequently requires more elaboration than do the other stages. Land and people of the so-called "New World" were epistemically, economically, and politically transformed into *things* and *property*. In this period, local European kingdoms became global land-lords, and local Indigenous Peoples became labor force and land-less. Regrettably, this configuration continues even five centuries later.

During this time, an infamous belief became cemented in the religious imagination of the peoples of the Americas, just like in the case of Rahab (Josh 2:8–11), except much more pronounced: *That God blesses the foreigner-in-power and tolerates the use of imperial violence to accomplish his purpose in our lands and peoples, and that this is corroborated by the victory of the European conquest.* As a result, the human profile of the *land-less* population remained relatively the same in the American Global South. Latin American countries and their immigrant progenies living in the Global North moved from being savages to barbarians to premodern

26. The following section elaborates on content I present in García-Johnson, *Spirit Outside the Gate*, 119–31.

27. García-Johnson, *Spirit Outside the Gate*, 109.

to undeveloped. The profile of *land-lords*, however, changed geopolitically in the ladder of the West: from Iberian powers to North Atlantic European powers to the United States of America. This latter represents a European prodigy of sorts, born in the context of American settlement and British bondage but self-liberated to ascend rapidly to the top of the ladder of world dominance, just as a geopolitical messiah would do.

During this period, the theology of the landlord and landless was indelibly inscribed in the geopolitical relationship of the colonizer-colonized of the American Global South. The natives (and enslaved Africans and everyone in between) became a commodity and orphans, a commodity because they were bought and sold, enslaved and exploited, and orphans because when "one loses one's land, which gives life and identity, especially a land that very particularly means motherhood (Pachamama), such a loss translates into being displaced, homeless, and an orphan."[28] Then comes the colonial rule established after 1570 and lasting until the political independence of the Latin American republics.

The colonial wound, in the form of a geopolitical subjugation that affected the very *humanitas* and *societas* of the peoples and lands of the Americas, was sealed during this period, on the basis of mission Christology: Christ is projected on the side of the royal powers and their colonial structures as a monarch "who is covered with gold and silver . . . and wearing royal crowns like kings of Spain."[29] On the other hand, and representing the human condition of the natives of the colonized land is "the Christ of the cross, of the death that conquers . . . 'the archetypal beggar . . . a compendium of mysteries and a sampler of humiliations" encrusted violently over the indigenous imagination.[30] Pachamama and the territories of *Anáhuac*, *Tahuantinsuyu*, and *Ayiti* became royal property, Ferdinand's lands, and the inhabitants of the colonies became everlastingly Ferdinand's poor children in need of civilizing evangelization and colonial control.

2. Salvation by US Americanism
(1900s)

After the political independence of the Latin American republics, the continent experienced the great European migration, and this added class and

28. García-Johnson, *Spirit Outside the Gate*, 114.

29. García-Johnson, *Spirit Outside the Gate*, 120.

30. Trinidad, "Christology, Conquista, Colonization," 60.

political heft to the creole elites and the aristocracy, exacerbating their power through their fight for independence and political autonomy in the newly formed republics. The introduction of western Protestantism weakened any colonial control of the Iberian powers and churches that was still in place. In addition, this local expression of Protestantism was instrumental in building the necessary epistemic, cultural, economic, and political structures that would later position the United States of America as the new leader of the American continent—both its lands and its peoples.

The Protestant influence in the making of modern Latin America (and the majority world for that matter) was a game changer. The First Protestant Congress in Latin America (Panamá, 1916) attempted to launch a dual process of *protestantization* and *democratization* of Latin America but failed due to several factors including an attempt to launch, theologically, the US doctrine of Panamericanism as a formula for the success of the Latin American society. The idea of *America for the Americans* as an anti-European colonial tactic, oriented by the idea of one great centralized political utopia, never became concretized in the vision of Simón Bolivar (South America) or the political society behind the Monroe Doctrine (North America). Nevertheless, a variety of powerful factors created a singularity in the American continent that bridged the possibilities of conceding (colonial) power and control to the United States of America, factors such as the Protestant propagation of Manifest Destiny ideology,[31] the initial success of US monopolies in the republics, US military superiority, and the political inexperience and fragility of the young independent republics.

By the turn of the twentieth century, we see various forms of US *Americanisms* exercising influence over the American continent through gradual economic penetrations, Protestant civilizing missions, military invasions and interventions, and an ascending geopolitical hegemony. The theology of the land in the Americas was never resolved by the revolution, leading to the political independence of the Latin American republics; it was merely re-dressed in a new colonial garment fashioned after the modern coloniality of US Americanism. The invented Latin American territory and peoples moved from being under colonial rule to being a modern nation state in an illusion of embracing the liberal democratic ideals and becoming fully

---

31. For instance, O'Sullivan argues for Manifest Destiny by theologizing its ideology. One of the biblical issues at its core is the "dominion mandate" (Gen 1:28). "Congressman Timothy Pillsbury of Texas argued in 1846 that Mexicans were not able to fulfill the dominion mandate, and since they could not, their lands were forfeited to those who could" (Wilsey *American Exceptionalism and Civil Religion*, 80–81).

autonomous peoples and territories. An image that captures this aspiration is the memorable essay "Nuestra América" (Our America, 1891) by the Cuban philosopher, poet and apostle of the Cuban revolution, José Martí.

Modern patriotic narratives and the idea of the modern citizen replaced the colonial space and identity of the subjects of the former colonial rule. Latin Americans' romantic embrace of the values of western liberal democracy and the persistent contempt for pre-Hispanic cultural indigeneity, ancestral wisdom, and especially respect of and care for Mother Earth forged a theology of the land that gave Latin American Protestants a Bible (a Living Christ over and against the death Christ of Colonial Roman Catholicism). It gave Latin American Roman Catholics a place in national aristocratic religion. And it gave the United States of America carte blanche to expand and build an epistemic machine to propagate US Americanism as the ideal way of building the state, the citizen, and Christian civility.

3. Salvation by the Doctrine of Development
(1930s–1960s)

During this period, many nations of Latin America received a high dose of conservative modernization (industrialization of substitution). The US Protestant missions advanced and cemented the evangelical experience. On the one hand, biblical literacy helped to increase literacy in Latin American, the magisterial principles of the Reformation made credible the *humanitas* of the former colonial subject, and Latin Americans were now invited (but still passively invited, not acting on their own) to be agents of missions, not only objects of missions. On the other hand, western Protestantism continued to prescribe the principles of liberal democracy (Eurocentrically), now under the shape of economic development and modernization. In addition, US Pentecostalism became a powerful mission movement, impregnating the evangelical imagination of Latin America with the fundamentalist-liberal split, a-political faith, US Manifest Destiny, and the ideology of righteous capitalist economy. A (evangelical) theology of the land could then be summarized by saying that: "our perfect land is in heaven; our best land for now, on earth, is the United States of America." A very popular Pentecostal hymn illustrates how landlessness fed the social imagination of many *evangélicos/as* in the Americas during this time:

//Jerusalén, que bonita éres,
calles de oro, mar de cristal//
  //Por esas calles yo quiero caminar
  calles de oro, mar de cristal//
//Jerusalem, how beautiful are you!
streets of gold, sea of glass.
  //On those streets I wish to walk,
  streets of gold, sea of glass//[32]

4. Salvation by Market Capitalism
(1970s–2000s)

During this period, a combination of global economies, political neoliberalism, the implosion of socialism, and military technology, among other things, framed the hegemony of the Unites States as a global shaping force, particularly in the Americas. The entire continent suffered from a homogenization in the politico-economic space that was led by neoliberalism. The flip side of this ubiquitous power of the US political and military economy in Latin American countries would be seen in massive migrations of Latin Americans to the mythical "North."

Unsurprisingly, we see a number of contesting theological voices and church movements emerging from within the United States (diaspora/minoritized theologies) and from without (Liberation theology, Integral Mission, Indigenous Christian theologies).

The emergence of such counterhegemonic voices represents a response to the hegemony of US monoculturism in economic, political, educational, technological, scientific, cultural, and religious terms. During this time, new theological voices protested the indifference of the western theological establishment toward the structural impoverishment of a whole continent, the asymmetric distribution of power and privilege into the hands of one nation, and the ineffectiveness of western theological reflection to deal with these issues.

At the risk of oversimplification, I suggest we can see here two main paths for theology and the church in the Americas: the first, that of most mainline Protestant denominations and many of the renewal movement churches, was to continue to uphold the dogmas and practices transplanted

32. Public domain: https://www.musica.com/letras.asp?letra=2201851.

to the Americas by western Protestantism/Pentecostalism/Roman Catholicism, albeit translated into their own particular languages, local cultures,
and spiritual preferences; the second, that of a sort of "ecclesiogenesis,"[33]
to use Leonardo Boff's concept of base ecclesial communities, that
erupted among some sectors of Roman Catholicism, mainline Protestantism, and creole Pentecostalism. In the case of Roman Catholicism, this
ecclesiogenesis is predominantly liberationist in character, while in the
case of mainline Protestantism we can call it "integral mission" and say
it is primarily missiological. In the case of creole Pentecostalism, we see
"neopentecostalism/church growth" erupting as the basis of local ecclesial
transformations. This latter points to a hybrid of ecclesial corporativism
with transnational and global reaches.

I group them together here simply on the basis of their response to
US monoculturalism during this period, but without providing a formal
critique of any of them. I do that elsewhere under the rubric "utopic gate:
coloniality of time and history."[34] But we can say that each of them represents a response to western monoculturalism, with respect to the church
and historical reality as experienced in the Global South. All of them use
their scriptural imagination to offer a response.

Diaspora theologies, such as US Latino/a theology, locate theological
analysis primarily in culture and propose cultural resistance on all fronts
(race, gender, class, politics, economics, etc.) to western monoculturalism,
and would do this analysis from within the US establishment.

Liberation theology locates theological analysis primarily in the historical process, initially, as this process was experienced in the class and economic struggles of the impoverished masses, and would thus propose historical
liberation (political, economic, social) on a scriptural basis.

Integral Mission (IM) locates resistance in the church itself as a social
agent of transformation. Integral Mission's idea of church is not, however,
the institutional church so much as a functional concept of self-awareness,
social consciousness, and missional deployment into the public space. In
short, advocates of IM think of the disciples of the kingdom of God in
terms of embracing their moral agency in society. They place the weight
of social transformation on incarnated missional action that ought to be
present in all spheres of life (Spanish: "integralidad"). This follows the

33. Boff, *Ecclesiogenesis.*
34. García-Johnson, *Spirit Outside the Gate*, 79–83.

incarnational model of mission action of Jesus of Nazareth that we see registered in the New Testament accounts.[35]

Finally, within Latin American Neopentecostalism, several leaders and churches assumed a sort of *Latin American Manifest Destiny* mindset or Latin American sense of "this is our time for expanding the kingdom of God to the whole world" in response to which they launched a generation of mega churches/ministries. Interestingly, although many of these churches and leaders are still affected by the colonial wound, their sense of evangelistic achievement and mission accomplishment does not follow the patterns established by western Christianity. On the contrary, it has influenced western Pentecostalism.[36]

In short, since the 1970s the various theologies of the land-lord and land-less in the context of the Americas have been shifting focus, with the result that different contesting voices, different biblical readings of social agency, and different missional and political agendas are finding a place at the table of public discourse like never before. The common trigger seems to be US monocultural Americanism as the hegemonic expression of the matrix of colonial power of our time. This suggests that US/western monoculturalism is currently in crisis, although it still continues to be hegemonic.

What can we say about the theology(ies) of the land in the Americas after this discussion?

1. A critical view of how theological cartographies informed the European conquest and the multiples colonial acts that construct what today we call America and/or Latin America shows that a *conquering* ethics together with an *othering* epistemic machine transformed Mother Earth (Pachamama) and ancient civilizations (enslaved Africans and Original Americans) into exploitable land, a labor force, and soteriological objects of European Christendom.

2. These transformations took specific shape in the making of *land-lords* and *land-less* populations in the Americas. This is basically the shape of theology of the land in the context of colonial and (neo)colonized America. In addition, this constitutes a global design that has been built up over five centuries and is now being contested by the subaltern

---

35. See Padilla, *Misión Integral*, 130–55.

36. On the rise of Indigenous Christian theologies, such as from Tinker, Kidwell, Woodley, Twiss, see the essay by a Cree scholar, Danny Zacharias, in this volume.

communities sharing modern-colonial-imperial subjugations of the American Global South.

3. The colonial wound, a set of infamous beliefs that give shape to the *humanitas* and *societas* of the lands and peoples of the Americas, became hardened during colonial rule and was re-opened by various colonial actors across different formation stages of the modern American continent. As a result, the profile of the *land-less* population has remained relatively unaltered, while the colonial *land-lords* have shifted from being Southern Europe to Northern Europe to the mythical "North" of America, the United States of America.

4. In the last fifty years, we have seen contesting voices emerge from the theological and ecclesial spheres of the American Global South and attempt to respond to the seemingly unstoppable and homogenizing force of US monoculturalism (in cultural, religious, economic, political, military, technological, scientific, and epistemic forms). All of these responses are valid, some of them are helpful, but most of them are insufficient to change the course of the epistemic/ethical machine of monoculturalism. Most of these responses attempt to recover the value of that humanity demolished at the conquest, subjected during colonial rule, and regulated during our modern history. The modern/colonial/occidental shell has proven to be inescapable to most of them, at least as regards their utopic imagination. For instance, Liberationist projects have attempted to liberate the land and the people on the basis of counterhegemonic modern paradigms (on the left), in an effort to recover and reshape the power of the modern nation state, in so doing leaning toward state-centrism. Many Neopentecostal movements have focused on changing political and economic frameworks, in so doing leaning toward neoliberalism. A common and dangerous idea is that the ecclesial sector can (re)gain political and financial leadership over the public or the private sector. In addition, many believe that a mega church could function as a "city of God" (theocratically). They also believe that under a righteous and anointed leadership together these elements would do the trick for a better society and national prosperity—meaning they would be more moral, equitable, and blessed thanks to clean (pious) profitmaking. This noble idea is not only naïve but also dangerous, given the long and devastating history of western Christendom. Finally, the idea that the church can function as a moral agent of social transformation, as Integral Mission has

maintained, is important but limited by the biblical imagination of the West that informs this view. It takes for granted that the church and the state are necessary pieces of social transformation and leaves very little room for non-modern/colonial structures (meaning specifically for indigenous communities and ancestral wisdoms), and Transmodern experiments in line with pluriversality and plurinationality.

Re-traditioning the Land:
Towards a Transamerican Theology

A theology of the land from a decolonial perspective ought to begin with the task of myth-busting. This requires subverting western epistemic normativity, which operates by whitening "truth, beauty, and good" in an effort to canonize (white heroes) and condemn (non-white *monsters*). Frantz Fanon summarizes this idea as follows: "Nxxxoes are savages, brutes, illiterate. But in my own case I knew that these statements were false. There was a myth of the Nxxxo that had to be destroyed at all cost[s]."[37]

Willie Jennings likewise articulates eloquently how the epistemic machine of colonial modernity re-shaped the meaning of lands and peoples of the Americas at the time of (and since) the European conquest, inviting an agenda for an otherwise theology of the land: "Everything—from peoples and their bodies to plants and animals, from the ground and the sky—was subject to change, subjects for change, subjected to change. The significance of this transformation cannot be overstated. The earth itself was barred from being a constant signifier of identity."[38] What would it take to re-signify Mother Earth (Pachamama) and the Original American theologically? Or perhaps this is the wrong starting point. Instead perhaps: What would it take to re-signify theology on the basis of an Original American trans-occidental imagination? I call this process re-traditioning.

Re-traditioning the Land as a Process of
De-monstrifying Indigenous Peoples

The re-signification of theology from the perspective of America otherwise conceived begins with a different positionality of the interpreter, one

37. Fanon, "The Fact of Blackness."

38. Jennings, *The Christian Imagination*, 43.

different to that upheld by those in the fifteenth to seventeenth centuries who "invented, mapped, appropriated, and exploited [America] under the banner of the Christian mission" through multiple colonial acts.[39] The point is not a return to an idyllic past or a golden age, a sort of unified indigenism that in reality never existed beyond the western anthropological imagination. The act of reimagining Americanity by self-positioning before and beyond coloniality/modernity/Occidentalism is also a self-discovery/uncovering of sorts. It is an act of re-traditioning the experience with the land on the basis of a liberative ecology. The social imaginary that produced the first epistemic transformations in the form of corporeal dis-embeddedness must be reconceived in a way that is able to uncouple itself from colonial logics, rhetorical modernities, and Occidentalizing languages. Colonial modernity and its epistemic machine has conceived of disembodied bodies, minds devoid of connection to the land and fictitious characters with an agenda in mind: to tell the story of pious western heroes in a land of evil non-western monsters, and to build global designs to promote them as universal truth.

We can literally see the fabrication of white western heroes in tandem with the monstrification of lands and peoples of the Americas through the history of colonial visual arts.[40] Three examples come to mind. First, the colonial travel literature genre as illustrated by Theodore de Bry's *Collected Travels in the East Indies and West Indies* (1590–1634), which ingeniously portrays—for the European public—the newly "discovered" lands as dominions of demons whose inhabitants are visually depicted as "uncivilized, unclothed, and pagan."[41]

Second, John Bulwer's *Anthropometamorphosis* (1650) uses elements of comparative cultural anthropology to depict the savagery and blasphemous

39. Mignolo, *The Darker Side of Western Modernity*, 6.

40. Daniele da Volterra's oil on slate "Le Combat de David et Goliath" (1550–1555) depicts a blond, light-skinned young man wielding a sword and standing over a dark-skinned, brown-haired, much larger man. Images such as the previously described fueled the fire of biblical Occidentalism. A noteworthy case is the most revered Spanish Bible version for Latin American evangelicos/as, The Reina-Valera 1960. In 1 Samuel 17:42, the Hebrew word *admoni* is translated as "rubio" (blond) to describe King David. A more accurate translation of *admoni* would be "trigueño" (ruddy). Songs of Solomon 5:10 reads, "Mi amado es blanco (*tsakh*) y rubio (*adom*)" (My beloved is white and blonde). A more accurate translation of the word *tsakh* would be "resplandecente" (dazzling). Also *adom* should be translated as "trigueño" (red, ruddy). The white norms in biblical languages is at high pitch here by fabricating a modern white hero from ancient biblical figures.

41. Kilroy-Ewbank, "Inventing 'America' for Europe: Theodore de Bry."

nature of Indigenous populations who exhibit tattoos and devil-inspired body piercing, in so doing contaminating and transforming the human bodies even of civilized Europeans who are in contact with them.

Third and finally, the *Casta* genre paintings that appeared in the early seventeenth century during the reign of Philip V, which point to the elites' loss of control of colonial cultural-racial power and to how they "participated in the construction of identity in New Spain, also contributed to the transmission of discourses of power within the Spanish empire as a whole."[42]

In short, all of these visual artefacts, though produced in different locations (Germany, England, Mexico, Perú), used sophisticated othering mechanisms through the inventive western process of cultural images together with their perceived categories of lands and peoples. The creators of such artefacts transformed lands and territories such *Anáhuac, Tahuantinsuyu,* and *Ayiti* into unoccupied, empty, ownable spaces ready for white western heroes and saviors to possess. These art samples document the process of monstrification of the Indigenous-other, a process that was necessary for the invention of the western-other as a redemptive figure whose colonial acts in the shape of conquest, colonization, (and later on) modernization, democratization, and economic development were to be considered ultimately pious and even biblically legitimate.

As a Christian decolonial epistemology, transoccidentality hopes to undo these stories by telling other stories from a different place.[43] Transoccidentality functions as an imaginary whose epistemic codes of human identity, and the cosmic self, organize at the border of the regime of coloniality/modernity/Occidentalism in the other America, Trans-Americanity. Transoccidentality points to Trans-Americanity as a form of inhabiting the "erasures of coloniality" (Mignolo) in an effort to de-monstrify the wounded American self that is inscribed in land and bodies. In other words, Trans-Americanity is an imagined geography too, and has theological cartography too, but is one produced not by the invading heroes of the West nor elaborated with the colonial grammar that writes the metanarratives of the land-lords but by the subaltern communities who share imperial/colonial/modern subjugations, namely, by the land-less.

42. Cline, "Guadalupe and the Castas," 170.

43. Likewise, some environmental critics are using the method of "re-storying" the earth by emphasizing "sacred life and living earth story" as a way to counteract colonial modernity and market economy portrayals of the earth as a natural resource at the service of "sacred money and market story." See Taylor, *Ecopiety,* 19–40.

Transoccidentality invites a new form of cartography of the American Self. And Trans-Americanity constitutes the set of geopolitical factors that give corporeal tissue and structure to that new American Self in such a way that the Zapatista dictum, for example, of "a world in which many worlds fit" can be realized. In this sense, it points to a corporeal theology of the people of "Nuestra America" (Our America), a decolonial cosmology with a liberative ecology, where Pachamama cannot be reduced to an ownable piece of dirt because She is alive, speaks, and takes care of us. And in return, we relate to her and care for her in an act of worship to God, in whom we all "live and move and have our being" (Acts 17:28, ESV). Of this an Andean Christian *campesino* (peasant) speaks with great theological competence and cosmological acumen when he says: "Pachamama is like a holy virgin that says to God: I will feed your children."[44] These words and its imagery can be also considered "canonical" to the peoples of "Nuestra America." Transoccidentality may help us create the "epistemological ground on which coherent versions of the world [all our worlds] may be produced."[45]

Re-traditioning the Land as Re-signifying Theology with Indigenous Content

I have argued that the "re-origination of Christian theology in Our Other America" (Trans-Americanity) should begin with the theology of Original Americans.[46] I have used decolonial pneumatologies (and challenged westernized christologies) as a theological discourse to dialogue with Indigenous sources in search of shared epistemic grounds. I have argued that the "Americas' theological borders are porous, nomadic and pluriversal, unveiling epistemic *mestizajes* that facilitate the transit of traditions and the embodiment of belief."[47] Consequently, any theo-*logic*—meaning any situated form of reasoning about God's interaction with creation—in such a context must operate from within, hence appreciating rather than discounting *a priori* what Indigenous theological traditions have to offer as an epistemic donation to the ecologies of knowledge.

A clear task for a *theo-logic-al* approach from within is to be able to map and critically analyze theological trajectories of embedded

44. Andean Christian Peasant in Marzal, *Tierra Encantada*.

45. Saldívar, *Trans-Americanity*, 56.

46. García-Johnson, *Spirit Outside the Gate*, 203.

47. García-Johnson, *Spirit Outside the Gate*, chap. 9.

rationalities (traditions) witnessing to the multiple perceptions of God, after, across, outside, and before the arrival of Christendom. I typically use three target communities in my research to document my analyses on traditioning communities in the Americas: Original Americans, Afro-Latinos/as, and immigrants of the South.[48] Here, I restricted my discussion to the Original Americans as I have elaborated the contours of a Transamerican theology elsewhere.

I have argued that "originating cultures' aesthetic and theological syntheses are original products of traditioning communities (or original christianities, if you will) exercising their own canonical imagination as opposed to western deviations (wicked and evil) finding judgement under the essentializing classifications" of western epistemic normativity (i.e., syncretism, Christopaganism).[49] Creation, place, space, and the land are all part of the primary ground (or spatiality) on and in which the experience of the Creator Spirit happens for Indigenous communities of the Americas as well as for other Indigenous communities on the planet. These are deeply theological themes in this Transoccidental epistemic horizon with the potential to re-route the theological process and recreate the theological agenda. In the words of the Osage Christian theologian George Tinker:

> Essentially, an American Indian theology must argue out of American Indian spiritual experience and praxis that Creator ("God"?) is revealed in creation, in space or place, and not in time . . . American Indian spirituality, values, social and political structures, and even ethics are rooted not in some temporal notion of history [the euro-western episteme], but in spatiality. This is perhaps the most dramatic, and largely unnoticed, cultural difference between American Indian thought processes and the western intellectual tradition.[50]

Yet for the re-traditioning of the Indigenous peoples' experience of the American land to occur in such a way that the theological process is re-originated, the process itself must be started from a different place, narrative, and spiritual community. This place and its community ought to be deeply interconnected so that the social imaginary retains the necessary ambiguity, polyvalence, and mestizo(a)logy that is required

48. García-Johnson, *Spirit Outside the Gate*, chap. 9. For an appealing argument in favor of Christian animism as the basis of ancient and post-modern Christianity, see Wallace, *When God Was a Bird*, 1–49.

49. García-Johnson, *Spirit Outside the Gate*, 191.

50. Tinker, *Spirit and Resistance* [Kindle Loc. 1475–76, 1492–94].

to subvert the disembodying western epistemic. Assisted by decolonial theorists, I call the *locus theologicus* from where this is possible the "colonial difference." Based on my research and elaboration of decolonial pneumatology, I identify the following elements as central for the construction of a Transamerican theology:

- **A liberative ecology.** The Transoccidental epistemology that informs Transamerican theology must first be disconnected from colonial modernity's "cosmology of domination."[51] As current critics of this dominant cosmology put it, "there is no single term that fully captures the cosmovision that currently holds sway over modern industrialized societies."[52] But some elements do adversely affect any proposal I or others make for a Transamerican theology. The elements of a dominant cosmology:[53] 1) separate mind and matters, bodies and consciousness as separate entities; 2) understand nature and the cosmos in mechanistic terms (determinism), which enables androcentric power structures to know all things and controls all knowledge by breaking it into/reducing it to its component parts; 3) consider that there is no purpose to nature and the cosmos; 4) believe the *uni*-verse to be eternal and immutable in nature; 5) believe that all life on earth is involved in a never-ending competition for survival. A Transamerican theology moves away from the understanding of colonial modernity' nation state (and thus a corporate capitalistic global design) as the owner of the land and the fiscal agent of its biodiversity and hence fully and autonomously functioning as a self-sufficient/self-ruling entity on ecological matter. A Transamerican theology moves towards concepts of nation states reformulated by a liberative ecology under the principle of bioregionalism. A liberative ecology under a bioregional model points to: "region/ community (scale), conservation/restoration stability/evolution/adaptation local/self-sufficiency cooperation primary (economy), decentralization complementarity/subsidiary diversity/consensus participation/ empowerment (policy), symbiosis evolution/qualitative growth plurality/diversity [transmodern pluriversality]."[54]

51. See Hathaway and Boff, *The Tao of Liberation*, chapter 6 [Kindle Loc. 3384].

52. Hathaway and Boff, *The Tao of Liberation*, Kindle Loc.3384.

53. Hathaway and Boff, *The Tao of Liberation*. Taken directly and sumarized from Kindle Loc. 3417.

54. Hathaway and Boff, *The Tao of Liberation*. Adapted from Kindle Loc. 8274.

- **A Gaia/Pachamama-Spirit covenantal theology.** A Transamerican theology acknowledges that the peoples of the American Global South are both recipients of multiple traditions as well as traditioning communities themselves.[55] In the same breath, a Transamerican theology views the land (Pachamama, Gaia) as alive, as part of the cosmos, and as deeply connected to the Spirit of God. The Spirit of God registers in the early creeds of the Eastern and Western Christian church as the life giver, the Spirit of Life. Beyond this East/West canonical registry, the Spirit of life is experienced as the Spirit of sustainability of the earth, the Spirit that dignifies the earth and is God's covenantal partner in the creation of humankind and other species. The Gaia/Pachamama-Spirit covenantal relationship is traceable in the Judeo-Christian biblical tradition (canonical imagination of the West), although it has hardly been accessed through that epistemic venue. For instance, we can see traces of this Gaia/Pachamama-Spirit of God covenantal relationship in Old Testament accounts where God's relationship with the earth discloses an unbreakable bond. This covenant relationship is not cosmocentric or androcentric but dialogical. As such, it includes the unbreakable bond between humankind and the earth. The priestly account of creation (Gen 1:28) places the 'ādām (humankind) as the crown jewel of creation and gives them dominion over it (the power of obedience to the natural processes and responsibility for mutual sustainability). In the Yahwist's account (Gen 2:7) the 'ādām is formed/made from the 'ādāmâ (earth). Then, God creates the garden and settles the 'ādām there. They are given the responsibility to work and administer the land. The so-called human disobedience in this narrative is inescapably linked to cosmic disharmony for which the characters of this story suffer "justifiable" displacement. Interestingly, we see the land (Gaia-Pachamama) alive and participating with God in the development of the events (Gen 3:8; 4:10). Even when the human characters of this story are displaced from their original sustainable habitat that Gaia/Pachamama and the Spirit of God provided, they resettled (Gen 3:24). The New Testament gives us illuminating registries about Gaia/Pachamama and the Son of God by means of stories that communicate a deep intimate relationship between Jesus of Nazareth and the earth.[56] Pauline and Johannine literatures account for the

---

55. García-Johnson, *Spirit Outside the Gate*, chaps. 7, 8, 9.

56. In Matt 8:26–27 Jesus rebukes the winds and the sea. However, the Greek word

Gaia/Pachamama covenantal partnership with God as the Eschaton unfolds (Rom 8:20–22;[57] Rev 21:1–8). Likewise, we find traces of the Gaia/Pachamama covenantal partnership in the canonical imagination of the Americas as witnessed by the traditioning communities of the American Global South. A Transamerican theology has the task and agenda of putting these canonical imaginations (West and Americas) into dialogue for mutual enrichment. Evidently, God's wider revelatory presence in the cosmos, conscience, and cultures demands nothing less than that.[58]

- **A wounded Christian imagination.** The recognition of our wounded Christianity is the very horizon where we see decolonial pneumatology in operation. My research found that newer forms of Christian missions and ecclesial traditions in the American Global South carry within themselves the colonial wound and seek to transcend it by attempting full-occidentalization and full-de-occidentalization, and by reverting to spiritualities that inhabit liminal spaces and allow for multiple epistemic universes to coexist. With this in mind, a Transamerican theology acknowledges that the Spirit of God has been present in the lands and peoples of the Americas before and beyond the colonial acts of the European conquest, colonization, modernization, and economic development, all of which have been underwritten by a westernized Christian rhetoric of salvation.[59] The Gaia/Pachamama-Spirit Covenantal partnership is an epistemic horizon in which the *Spirit Outside the Gate* is a nomad and decolonial healer who abides *not in time* but, for instance, among the Original American people in their stories, songs, prayers, ceremonies—all rooted deeply in

---

epitimaō, translated as "rebuke," directly means "to warn by instructing." Although "rebuke" is not necessarily wrong, its basic sense is "to warn to prevent something from going wrong." Here Jesus exemplifies the possibility for redemption of the relationship between humanity and creation. The curse over the land (Gen 3:17), because of the first Adam, can be lifted because of the second Adam. See also Matt 21:18–22; Mark 4:35–41; Luke 8:22–25.

57. "For the creation was subjected to *futility*" (v. 20) In the Greek, the word is *mataiotés*, here rendered as "futility," implies *purposelessness, no meaningful end*, or *aimlessness*. The remaining verses, 21 and 22, go on to describe the end of that "aimlessness" of creation, which includes the land, once God delivers it from the corruption of sin brought about by humankind, see Gen 3:17.

58. See Johnston, *God's Wider Presence*.

59. García-Johnson, *Spirit Outside the Gate*, chap. 7.

Grandmother, the earth, as "their ways of life revere" creation and the Creator, believing that their stories will ultimately heal and "win over the immigrant conquerors and transform them."[60] Also, the Gaia/Pachamama-Spirit Covenantal partnership is expressed in the Yoruba-Christian spiritualities of the Afro-Latinos/as with respect to the living relationship with the ancestors, who have been buried in the earth but are somehow alive (under a different set of circumstances) because Gaia/Pachamama is alive. The same applies to the prominent celebration of El Día de Los Muertos, an Indigenous Mesoamerican Christian ceremony popular mostly among Latinx Roman Catholics.

- **An ethic of recognition-assemblage-decolonial healing.** A Transamerican theology is predicated on a Transoccidental epistemology as well as an ethic that orients the epistemic and utopic agenda from the start. As I have argued in "The Politics of the *Espíritu*," the ethical task in the context of subaltern communities sharing modern-colonial-imperial subjugations aims at world sustainability and "is not sectional, lineal, or even progressive but involves intersectionality, simultaneousness, multi-chronic logics (dealing with the multiple historical layers of reality embodied in the communities). Thus, as one deals ethically with the current conditions of cultural disintegration, one must also map "spatialities, views of the self, and epistemologies" that contribute to a delinking from wounding colonial narratives, and simultaneously provide an "incarnational imagination" of corporeal assemblage [lands, peoples, biodiversity], while exercising decolonial sociopolitical practices or tactics as a counternarrative to the hegemonic colonial modernity world-systems. This matrix of sociopolitical resistance of the *Espíritu* has been present in various ways since day one of the European conquest and is identifiable in communities such as Original Indigenous Americans, Afro-Latinxs, and more recently, immigrants of the South."[61] These subaltern communities' five hundred years of vicarious colonial sacrifice and decolonial resistance are the great ecological donations to the making of an ethic of care and liberative cosmologies, theologies, political economies, sciences, technologies, and societies.

---

60. Tinker, *Spirit and Resistance*, Kindle loc. 1638–40.
61. García-Johnson, "The Politics of the *Espíritu*," 366.

May the vicarious sacrifice and resistance of the American Global South,

that "large set of creations and creatures that have been sacrificed

to the infinite voracity of capitalism, colonialism, patriarchy,"[62]

be taken into account for the making of a Transamerican theology of the land:

a mystical and re-enchanted vision of the world where heaven and earth,

and all the elements that come from this marriage, operate under another logic,

at the erasures of coloniality/modernity/Occidentalism.

Trans-Americanity it is.

In the Power of the Spirit Outside the Gate,

the Covenant Partner of Pachamama,

we pray, Amen.

Further Reading

Dyrness, William A., and Oscar García-Johnson. *Theology without Borders: An Introduction to Global Conversations.* Grand Rapids: BakerAcademic, 2015.

Dussel, Enrique. *Invention of the Americas: Eclipse of the "Other" and the Myth of Modernity.* Translated by Michael D. Barber. New York: Continuum, 1995.

Medina, Néstor. "The Doctrine of Discovery, LatinXo Theoethics, and Human Rights." *Journal of Hispanic/Latino Theology* 21 (2019) 157–73. https://repository.usfca.edu/jhlt/vol21/iss2/4.

Moraña, Mabel., et al. eds. *Coloniality at Large: Latin America and the Postcolonial Debate.* Latin America Otherwise. Durham: Duke University Press, 2008.

Segovia, Fernando F., and Stephen D. Moore, eds. *Postcolonial Biblical Criticism: Interdisciplinary Intersections.* Bible and Postcolonialism. London: T. & T. Clark, 2005.

Bibliography

Boff, Leonardo. *Ecclesiogenesis: The Base Communities Reinvent the Church.* Translated by Robert R. Barr. Maryknoll, NY: Orbis, 1986.

Brunstetter, Daniel R., and Dana Zartner. "Just War against Barbarians: Revisiting the Valladolid Debates between Sepúlveda and Las Casas." *Political Studies* 59 (2011) 733–52.

62. Santos, *Epistemologies of the South*, 2.

Cline, Sarah. "Guadalupe and the Castas: The Power of a Singular Colonial Mexican Paint-ing." *Mexican Studies* 31 (2015) 218–47.

Dyrness, William A., and Oscar García-Johnson. *Theology without Borders: An Introduction to Global Conversations.* Grand Rapids: Baker Academic, 2015.

Espín, Orlando O. *Idol and Grace: On Traditioning and Subversive Hope.* Maryknoll, NY: Orbis, 2014.

Ezigbo, Victor Ifeanyi, and Reggie L. Williams. "Converting a Colonialist Christ: Toward an African Postcolonial Christology." In *Evangelical Postcolonial Conversations: Global Awakenings in Theology and Praxis*, edited by Kay Higuera Smith, Jayachitra Lalitha, and L. Daniel Hawk, 88–103. Downers Grove, IL: InterVarsity Academic, 2014.

Fanon, Frantz. "The Fact of Blackness." In *Postcolonial Studies: An Anthology.* Edited by Pramod Nayar. Wiley Blackwell, 2016. Kindle edition.

García-Johnson, Oscar. "The Politics of the *Espíritu*: Ethic as Recognition-Assemblage-Decolonial Healing." In *T&T Clark Handbook of Political Theology*, edited by Rubén Rosario Rodríguez, 355–72. New York: T. & T. Clark, 2019.

———. *Spirit Outside the Gate: Decolonial Pneumatologies of the American Global South.* Downers Grove, IL: InterVarsity Academic, 2019. Kindle edition.

Grosfoguel, Ramón. "The Structure of Knowledge in Westernized Universities: Epistemic Racism/Sexism and the Four Genocides/Epistemicides of the Long 16th Century." *Human Architecture: Journal of the Sociology of Self-Knowledge* 11.1 (2013), Article 8. https://scholarworks.umb.edu/humanarchitecture/vol11/iss1/8.

Hathaway, Mark, and Leonardo Boff. *The Tao of Liberation: Exploring the Ecology of Transformation.* Maryknoll, NY: Orbis, 2009.

Hidalgo, Jacqueline M. *Revelation in Aztlán: Scriptures, Utopias, and the Chicano Movement.* New York: Palgrave Macmillan, 2016.

Jennings, Willie James. *The Christian Imagination: Theology and the Origins of Race* New Haven: Yale University Press, 2010.

Johnston, Robert K. *God's Wider Presence: Reconsidering General Revelation.* Grand Rapids: Baker Academic, 2014.

Koschorke, Klaus et al., eds. *A History of Christianity in Asia, Africa, and Latin America, 1450–1990: A Documentary Sourcebook.* Grand Rapids: Eerdmans, 2007.

Kilroy-Ewbank, Lauren. "Inventing 'America' for Europe: Theodore de Bry." *Khan Academy.* https://www.khanacademy.org/humanities/art-americas/british-colonies/colonial-period/a/inventing-america-for-europe-theodore-de-bry.

Marzal, Manuel M. *Tierra Encantada: Tratado de Antropología Religiosa de América Latina*, Colección Estructuras y Procesos. Madrid: Pontifica Universidad Católica de Perú/Editorial Trotta, 2002.

McFarland Taylor, Sarah. *Ecopiety: Green Media and the Dilemma of Environmental Virtue.* New York: New York University Press, 2019.

Medina, Néstor. *Christianity, Empire and the Spirit: (Re)Configuring Faith and the Cultural.* Theology and Mission in World Christianity 11. Leiden: Brill, 2018.

Mignolo, Walter D. *The Darker Side of the Renaissance: Literacy, Territoriality, & Colonization.* 2nd ed. Ann Arbor: University of Michigan Press, 2003.

———. *The Darker Side of Western Modernity: Global Futures, Decolonial Options.* Durham: Duke University Press, 2011.

Padilla, C. René. *Misión Integral: Ensayos sobre el Reino de Dios y la Iglesia.* Buenos Aires: Kairos, 2012.

Pope Alexander VI. "*Inter Caetera*: Division of the Undiscovered World between Spain and Portugal." *Papal Encyclicals*, May 4, 1493.

Raheb, Mitri. *Faith in the Face of Empire: The Bible through Palestinian Eyes*. Maryknoll, NY: Orbis, 2014.

Saldívar, José David. *Trans-Americanity: Subaltern Modernities, Global Coloniality, and the Cultures of Greater Mexico*. New Americanists. Durham: Duke University Press, 2011.

Santos, Boaventura de Sousa. *Epistemologies of the South: Justice against Epistemicide*. Boulder, CO: Paradigm, 2014.

Smichtt, Carl. *The Nomos of the Earth: In the International Law of the Jus Plubicum Europaeum*. Candor: Telos, 2006.

Stahler-Sholk, Richard. "A World in Which Many Worlds Fit: Zapatista Responses to Globalization." In *XXII International Congress*. Presented at the Globalization in the New Millennium? Perspectives from/for Latin America, Miami, Florida: Latin American Association (LASA), 2000. http://lasa.international.pitt.edu/Lasa2000/Stahler-Sholk.PDF.

Tinker, George E. *Spirit and Resistance: Political Theology and American Indian Liberation* Minneapolis: Fortress, 2004. Kindle edition.

Trinidad, Saúl. "Christology, Conquista, Colonization." In *Faces of Jesus: Latin American Christologies*, edited by José Miguez Bonino, 57–62. Translated by Robert R. Barr. Maryknoll, NY: Orbis, 1984.

Valdeón, Roberto A. *Translation and the Spanish Empire in the Americas*. Benjamins Translation Library. Philadelphia: Benjamins, 2014.

Wallace, Mark I. *When God Was a Bird: Christianity, Animism, and the Re-Enchantment of the World*. New York: Fordham University Press, 2019.

Wilsey, John D. *American Exceptionalism and Civil Religion: Reassessing the History of an Idea*. Downers Grove, IL: InterVarsity Press, 2015.

Yugar, Theresa. "Letter to Eva." In *Voices from the Ancestors: Xicanx and Latinx Spiritual Expressions and Healing Practices*, 341–42. Tucson: University of Arizona Press, 2019.

3

The Land Takes Care of Us

Recovering Creator's Relational Design

H. Daniel Zacharias

Abstract

Despite common Christian discourse on environmental stewardship and creation care, a careful reading of the biblical text from
an intercultural framework shows that humanity is part of the
community of creation, not above it. Furthermore, we are placed
into a relationship of reciprocity with the land, with whom which
we are the one's cared for. The biblical portrait of our relationship with land is one of inter-dependence and inter-relatedness.
This relationship into which humanity is placed evidences itself
in several places within the Scriptures and can be understood as
a triangulation of relationship between God, humanity, and non-
human creation. This exegetical work has important theological
implications in building theologies of land and place.

Introduction

IMAGINE THIS SCENARIO: WE all wake up tomorrow after a good night's rest
and open our window shades to discover that all vegetation is gone. Every
tree dead and withered. Every plant, every blade of grass. We walk outside
in disbelief and here no sound. The insects are dead, there are no birds, no

squirrels. As panic sets in, we realize that all biotic life across the globe—in land, sea, and sky—is gone, with the exception of humans. How long would we as a species last? For some it would be a few weeks, for others a few months. But inside of a year, we would all perish.[1]

Now let's imagine a second scenario: the sun rises on a new day, but all of the humans are gone. Our household pets are the first ones to notice, along with zoo animals and other injured animals under permanent care. How long would the rest of non-human creation last without us? In scenario two, the situation is very different. Non-human creation—animals, birds, bugs, plants—would not only survive without us, but by all accounts would flourish.[2]

These two imaginative scenarios ought to sober our thinking, our language, and our actions toward non-human creation. Even the most environmentally-minded Christian thinkers and publications routinely use the language of "environmental stewardship" or "creation care."[3] With this type of language, an anthropocentric and hierarchical understanding of humanity's relationship to non-human creation continues. The modern evangelical discourse needs to be reformed because the models of creation care and environmental stewardship remain limited and based upon an anthropocentric theology. Richard Bauckham's work summarizes the critiques of the stewardship model as: 1) hubristic, 2) excluding God's own activity in the world, 3) lacking specific content, 4) setting humanity above creation rather than within it, and 5) the model isolates one passage of scriptural text (Gen 1:26, 28).[4]

Description ought to move from "creation care" by humanity to "creation's care" for humanity. There has not and will not be a time when humanity gives more to the creation than it has given and continues to give to us. The remainder of this essay will present a reading of the text from my perspective as an Indigenous follower of Jesus, formed as I am by my relations. This perspective is important for the global church in a warming world: "there is an urgent need for the Western church to

1. A similar scenario of creation undone occurs in Jer 4:23–28.

2. These two imaginative scenarios were in part sparked by Richard Bauckham's statement: "Whatever the rest of creation may need from us, it is certainly not the tyranny of pretended divine power. I have long found the question 'why should the rest of creation need us?' the hardest question about the meaning of the Genesis dominion and the human relationship to the non-human creation," in Bauckham, *Bible and Ecology*, 10.

3. A most recent example is Moo and Moo, *Creation Care*.

4. Bauckham, *Bible and Ecology*, 1–36.

recognize integrated constructs that encompass reciprocal relationships and the well-being of all things . . . Perhaps engaging the biblical witness from an Indigenous perspective can help Western Christians do this."[5] Intentionally leaning into an intercultural reading of the biblical text helps to understand how the Creator defines humanity's relationship to the rest of the community of creation.[6] The design of the Creator for this community is inter-relatedness and inter-dependence, and is set within a triangulation of relationship.

A Relational Reading of Genesis 1:1–2:4

An anthropocentric reading of the creation narrative in Gen 1:1—2:4 is fairly commonplace in both the academy and the church and is supported by modern printings of the text. It is well recognized that the very first chapter division of the Bible is poorly placed, as the seven day creation story is not completed until Gen 2:3 (or, as I will suggest, 2:4). Yet the very first verse of our sacred text makes it clear that Creator is the source of all things: "he is the grammatical subject of the first sentence and the thematic subject throughout the creation account."[7] The conclusion of the seven-day creation story with God's sabbath rest further pushes against an anthropocentric reading. In addition to the focus rightly on Creator, Indigenous readers and others have recognized the centrality of the earth within the narrative: "the primary subject of the primordial setting and subsequent days of creation was not the entire cosmos, nor humanity, but *erets*, Earth."[8] As is well established, the days of creation follow the pattern of creating the place or habitat (the sky, the water, the land) and then filling those places with occupants (the celestial bodies,

5. Woodley, "Early Dialogue in the Community of Creation," 93.

6. The description "community of creation" can be traced back to Jürgen Moltmann and has been utilized by Richard Bauckham and Randy Woodley. Bauckham, *Living with Other Creatures*; Moltmann, *God in Creation*; Woodley, *Shalom and the Community of Creation*. Woodley's work in particular shows that, while the precise description may not have been used in early Indigenous cultures, the concept of inter-relatedness and inter-dependence is foundational to the worldview of many Indigenous nations. The description resonates deeply with an Indigenous perspective on creation and, as will be shown, provides a more accurate relational description of the biblical data.

7. Martin, *Bound for the Promised Land*, 33–34. As noted by Wallace, "Rest for the Earth?," 50, the only exception to this is the seventh day, as that day does not begin with God as the subject.

8. Habel, "Geophany," 35.

aquatic creatures, land creatures—which includes humanity).[9] Through the days of creation, there is a basic pattern of God issuing forth a command for something to be created or to come forth, which is then followed by God either creating the thing commanded, and/or naming the created thing, and/or placing the created thing into its functional position. In all cases, the work is theocentric, with God issuing the command and then God completing the command, either implicitly or explicitly.

Command	Response
"Let there be light" (v. 3)[10]	God separates light from dark (v. 4) God names light day and darkness night (v. 5)
"Let there be a dome in the middle of the waters" (v. 6)	God made the dome (v. 7) God names the dome sky (v. 8)
"Let the waters under the sky come together into one place so that the dry land can appear." (v. 9)	God named the dry land earth, and the waters seas (v. 10)
"Let the earth grow plant life" (v. 11)	The earth produced plant life (v. 12)
"Let there be lights in the dome of the sky to separate the day from the night" (v. 14–15)	God makes the stars, sun, and moon (v. 16) God places them in the sky to rule the day and night (v. 17–18)
"Let the waters swarm with living creatures and let birds fly above the earth up in the dome of the sky" (v. 20)	God creates the sea creatures and birds (v. 21)
"Let the earth produce every kind of living thing" (v. 24)	God makes every kind of creature (v. 25)
"Let us make humanity" (v. 26)	God creates humanity (v. 27)

9. Walton, *Genesis*, 65.

10 Unless otherwise noted, all translations are from the Common English Bible (CEB).

The table above shows the issuing of the commands and their subsequent fulfillment. We see, for example, the created thing given a job: the celestial bodies are to rule over the day and night (1:18), and the marine creatures are commanded to be fertile and fill the seas, and the birds to fill the sky (1:22). A clear pattern is in the text: the gift of being created by God includes a sphere in which the created thing occupies and fulfills its responsibility, with the sphere itself being incomplete until it is fulfilling its function for the inhabitants. This gift establishes a reciprocity, with the celestial bodies performing their proper function, and marine and sky creatures being fertile. For all created things, to fulfill their responsibility is to obey the command of their Creator as a continual act of praise and reciprocity.

Given this pattern, it is important not to miss one extremely important break from the established pattern. Day three completes the creation of the inhabitable spaces and is also the first day that has a second act of creation. On day three, as expected, God issues forth a command beginning in v. 11:

> God said, "Let the earth grow plant life: plants yielding seeds and fruit trees bearing fruit with seeds inside it, each according to its kind throughout the earth." And that's what happened. *The earth produced* plant life: plants yielding seeds, each according to its kind, and trees bearing fruit with seeds inside it, each according to its kind. God saw how good it was. (1:11–13, CEB)

Whereas in all other instances God gives the command and then God explicitly or implicitly is the one who fulfills the command, in this verse it is mother earth herself that actively obeys the command by producing plant life.[11] The land here is described as a participant, or co-creator, in the creation of vegetation.[12] Like the other created things, which have reciprocated the gift of being created with fulfilling their function, the land also does so. This is not to elevate mother earth alongside the Creator. For instance, the account makes use of a different verb to describe the land's act of production in both vv. 12 and 24. But the co-creative power of ʾ *ereṣ*

---

11. The Hebrew nouns used to refer to the land are all feminine (ʾ*ădāmâ,* ʾ*ereṣ, yabbāšâ*), as are the Greek equivalents in the LXX (*gē, chōra*). More than that, though, is my attempt to heighten the relational language with which we talk about the land. The limitations of the English language is such that pronouns that are often confined for humans are restricted in their usage, and are very seldom applied outside of the animal kingdom. "The arrogance of English is that the only way to be animate, to be worthy of respect and moral concern, is to be a human" (Kimmerer, *Braiding Sweetgrass,* 57).

12. Habel, "Geophany," 34, states that "Earth and Elohim are both characters with major roles to play."

(land) is certainly clear from the Hiphil stem of *yṣ'* (to bring), emphasizing the causative force of the subject.[13] In contrast, when God's creative work is narrated, *'śh* (to make) is the verb used (1:7, 16, 25, 26). The language of co-creator is appropriate and should cause no concern, as other created things are also invited into the co-creation process through the function of reproduction (1:22, 28).[14] And while the co-creation language is most explicit in this instance, the co-creative connection on the sixth day with the creation of wild animals is certainly implied with the same verb *yṣ'* in the Hiphil being used, and the wild animals created are called "living earth creatures" (*hā 'āreṣ nepeš*) in 1:24.[15] The co-creation of vegetation in 1:12 is very important to recognize, as the vegetation from the third day is spoken of again on the sixth day. God gives this co-created vegetation as food for everything that breathes: humanity, wildlife, buglife, and birdlife (1:29–30). It is the land that provides, a gift given by the good Creator.

Interdependence within Creation

The establishment of interdependence within the community of creation occurs clearly within the seven days of creation, as created things through the seven days become increasingly dependent upon what has been created previously, particularly the place of habitation, and all things are ultimately dependent upon God.

> Each part of creation is differentiated, unique and fruitful, multiplying after its own kind. And yet, each part is incomplete without the whole; everything exists in interdependent relationships. The celestials regulate the balance of the terrestrials. The night compels all creation to rest as it brings refreshing coolness. The day provides new life and opportunities like warmth for plants, animals, and humans. The moon regulates the water. The sun regulates the seasons. The seasons regulate annual activities. Everything is in harmony, in balance with each other and with the creator. It is a picture of a creation in community, a picture in which the audience is being asked to see both the beauty and symmetry of many parts in relation to the whole.[16]

13. Koehler and Baumgartner, "*yṣ'*," 426.

14. See, for example, the reactionary statement against a co-creator reading in Mathews, *Genesis 1—11:26*, 152.

15 Noted also by Habel, "Geophany," 43.

16. Woodley, "Early Dialogue," 97–98.

In Genesis, the land animals, including humanity, are dependent upon a hospitable land to live and the gift of food provided by the land in Gen 1:30.[17] It is at this point when the interdependence among living creatures and the land is most clearly stated, and it is at this point that God saw that it was "very good" (Gen 1:31). Anthropocentric readings of the text often presume that the "very good"-ness being proclaimed is because now, at last, humanity has arrived on the scene. But the pronouncement follows upon God seeing "everything he had made," not just one particular portion of the created order. Perhaps the declaration of being "very good" is that now the creation exists in interdependence and harmony.[18] It is this aspect of dependence on the land and its gifts to humanity in particular that is picked up within the complementary creation story of Genesis 2. The word "gift" does not occur in the creation story, but the language of giving does, with ntn (to give) being used in 1:29–30 (see also Gen 9:3).

As has become increasingly clear thanks to the helpful work of John Barclay, the notion of pure gift is relatively absent in the ancient world.[19] Gifts initiated a relationship of reciprocity in the ancient world. This reciprocation happens in Eden, as humanity is placed in the garden to serve and conform to the land.[20] Because of the common western readings and translations of Gen 2:15, the land has been objectivized, resulting in a non-relational translation like the ESV's "to work (or till) it and keep it."[21] Yet the verb ʿbd is often translated as "to serve" and better conveys the reciprocal relationship established by God between humanity and the land.[22] The second verb is šmr. While "keep" is the most frequent choice of

17. Terence Fretheim states, "God has shaped the created order in such a way that there are overlapping spheres of interdependence and creative responsibility shared between Creator and creature. Moreover, the creatures are interdependent among themselves." See Fretheim, "Creator, Creature, and Co-Creation in Genesis 1–2," 15.

18. This point is also made by Richard Bauckham, see Bauckham, *Bible and Ecology*, 15. This very goodness, rather than being just ontological statements, seems to refer to the good functioning of all things. This fits with the usage of *ṭôb* (see Stoeber, "*ṭôb*," 487), and coincides with the functional view of John Walton, as espoused in Walton, *Lost World of Genesis*.

19. Barclay, *Paul and the Gift*, especially chap. 1 (pp. 11–65).

20. In a forthcoming article, Mark Brett and I will make the case that the best translation of Gen 2:15 is "to serve her and conform to her" (Brett and Zacharias, "To Serve Her and Be Conformed to Her.")

21. The modern translation that comes closest to the relational framing in the text is the NET translation, "to care for it and to maintain it."

22. See the note in HALOT that the Hebrew verb with *l* means "to work for someone,

translators, "keep" in modern English no longer conveys the same sense inherent in the word. This word is used specifically in the context of covenant discussions in the Mosaic Law that suggests a different nuance of the word here.[23] In many examples, almost always in a covenantal context, "to keep" these things is to conform one's life and actions to something. In the Mosaic law, the call is not just to know the commandments, not simply to conserve them, but to order their lives around them. Regardless of the English words used as glosses, the Hebrew words intimate a more relational understanding, and is framed within the Creator's establishment of ongoing reciprocal relationships. The land takes care of us, the Creator has deemed it to be so. And because of these gifts we receive from the land, and our utter reliance upon these gifts, humanity is to do its best to reciprocate in service and conformation.

While it is clear that humanity is the more dependent within the circle of relationship, yet the creation narrative also makes clear that there is a measure of dependence upon humanity for creation to flourish as the Creator intends. I will say more on this below when I discuss the *imago Dei*, but I do want to note the similarity in the creation narrative when it discusses the absence of humans. While it was not good for the human to be alone in Gen 2:18, it was first not good for the earth to be alone in Gen 2:5–8, as the service to the land by humanity displays the inter-dependency with the land.[24] The present reality that humanity is the greatest threat to the environment and to other members of the community of creation stands in stark contrast to Creator's intent.

---

serve," Koehler and Baumgartner, "'*bd*," 1:773. Note also Gen 4:12 and the disharmony within the established reciprocity because of Cain's sin. The choice of "serve" is furthered strengthened by the recognition that Eden is sacred space, see Walton, *Lost World of Genesis*, 70.

23. Some examples: In Gen 17:9, God tells Abraham "you must keep my covenant"; Throughout Exodus in the law, the Israelites are told to "keep" the feasts (Exod 12:17), to "keep" customs (Exod 12:25) to "keep" commands and statutes (Exod 13:10; 16:28), to "keep" the Sabbath (Exod 31:13–16). These are but a few examples of over 200 times that the word is used.

24. Habel also points out this conditional parallel, as the earth is also on its own (*tōhû wā bōhû*) and without interdependent relationships at the beginning of the seven-day creation story. See Habel, "Geophany," 38.

Interrelatedness within Creation

For a label like "community of creation" to be relevant, and for a statement like "the land takes care of us" to be accurate, establishment of not only inter-dependence but inter-relatedness is appropriate and necessary. The creation narrative bears this relatedness out in several ways. As Bauckham states, "the *fundamental* relationship between humans and other creatures is their common creatureliness . . . we, like them, are creatures of God. To lift us out of creation and so out of our God-given embeddedness in creation has been the great ecological error of modernity."[25] The relatedness of humanity with the land is emphasized in the word *ʾădām* for the first human, and *ʾădāmâ* for the ground—or as Robert Alter has translated, "humans" were made from "humus."[26] A further emphasis is placed on the "earthiness" of the first human by the specific usage of *ʿāpār*, topsoil, from which the first human is formed.[27] This word specifies the fertile topsoil, with all its wriggling worms, decayed matter, and fungul filaments. The living soil, which has always been vital for producing fruitful plants, is the soil from which humanity is also made. This reinforces the common creatureliness and kinship with the rest of creation and reminds the reader once again of the essential connection between humanity and the land. This essential connection exists also between other land creatures, as they are described as "living earth creatures" in 1:24. Traditional Indigenous culture and spirituality continues to emphasize practices that remind one of common creatureliness as well as connection to land, to remind oneself that you have been made from the land on which you and fellow creatures now walk and therefore have a kinship with them and with mother earth.[28]

The relatedness with animals, birds, and bugs is also highlighted by the mutual dependence upon the plants for sustenance (1:30). The declaration of God in 1:30 is also interesting in that every creature, including humanity, is described as those that have the breath of life (*nepeš ḥayyâ*) in them. This description groups humanity in common creatureliness and is the same description used for land animals (1:24), and sea creatures (1:20–21). This common description ought to caution readers against an

25. Bauckham, *Living with Other Creatures*, 4; italics his.

26. Alter, *The Five Books of Moses*, 21.

27. Stoeber, "*ʿāpār*," 939.

28. One example from the Aboriginal peoples of Australia is the frequent call to take off one's shoes when in the outdoors to renew your connection with the land and remind you that you are the land.

over-emphasized anthropocentric reading of the same description later applied to the human in 2:7.[29] So, too, humanity shares common crea-tureliness with the fish and birds in that they are also commanded to be fruitful and multiply (1:22), and the interrelatedness of the whole creation is also highlighted on the Sabbath day in 2:1, with the heavens and the earth being the common home to all.[30]

The capstone on the issue of inter-relatedness comes at the conclusion of the seven-day creation story in Gen 2:4a. Most English translations see the conclusion of the first creation story at 2:3, with 2:4 beginning the next creation story. Yet some translations, the CEB and the NRSV in particular, have presented 2:4a as the close of the first creation story, and 2:4b as the beginning of the second creation story. There are good literary reasons for doing so. The sentence provides an ideal bookend with 1:1, using the same verb *br'* (to create) for the act of creation. This verb is used five more times in the seven-day creation story (1:21, 27 [x3]; 2:3), but is not used in the complementary creation story of chapter 2. So too does "heaven and earth" form a bookend with Gen 1:1. At the word level, the demonstrative *'ēlle* can point either forwards or backwards depending on the context.[31] So too can the word *tôlēdôt* sit at the end of a genealogical record or at the beginning.[32] Robert Alter also notes the envelope structure created with 1:1 and 2:4a, noting that afterwards the style changes sharply.[33] This data I think leans towards seeing 2:4a as the end of the first creation story, or at the very least it is to see 2:4 as a transitionary verse which serves to bind the seven-day creation story with the focus on the creation of the human pair in Genesis 2, so it both closes the first part and opens the next.[34] Furthermore, the idea of

29. A canonical and synthesized reading of these texts should lead readers to the conclusion that God breathes the breath of life in all creatures, not just uniquely into humanity.

30. Wallace, "Rest for The Earth," 52. Randy Woodley notes that the Rainbow Spirit elders of Australia say, "the Creator sang on the seventh day, meaning there was a com-munity gathering where celebration was the only priority." See Woodley, "Early Dia-logue," 98.

31. Koehler and Baumgartner, "'ēlle," 52.

32. The word sits at the end of a genealogical record in Gen 10:32, Exod 6:19; 1 Chr 7:4, 9; 8:28; 9:1, 34.

33. "Instead of the symmetry of parataxis, hypotaxis is initially prominent: the sec-ond account begins with elaborate syntactical subordination in a long complex sentence that uncoils all the way from the second part of verse 4 to the end of verse 7." Alter, *Genesis*, 7 n. 4.

34. This complementary reading of Genesis 1 and 2 is held by a number of

kinship inherent in this verse does not cease at the close of the seven day account, but continues into the Genesis 2 account: "the human belongs to the same kinship group as the animals in the sense that they all descend from the land. In the genealogical terms suggested by the introductory formula in Gen. 2.4a . . . the land is the parent."[35] This provides further biblical support for the relational way I and fellow Indigenous peoples refer to the land as mother earth.

With all this in mind, the word *tôlēdôt* and its implications for all creation's inter-relatedness becomes clear. The word is clearly a relational concept, yet many translations de-emphasize the relational notion, using words like "account." Another frequent choice of "generations" gets closer to the idea, and the LEB (Lexham Press's pedantic translation available only digitally) suggests in a footnote, "these are the family records of the heavens and the earth." In a similar vein, *HALOT* (*Hebrew and Aramaic Lexicon of the Old Testament*) includes Gunkel's suggestion of "this is the family tree of the heaven and the earth as they were created."[36] While *HALOT* ultimately does not endorse Gunkel's suggestion, his suggestion is faithful to the use of the word, its root form *yld* (to beget), and the theology of Genesis 1. This fits well with an intercultural reading of the text and aligns with Indigenous creation stories: "connectedness positions individuals in sets of relationships with other people and with the environment. Many Indigenous creation stories link people through genealogy to the land, to the stars, and other places in the universe, to birds and fish, animals, insects and plants."[37] In practice, some First Nations of North America use the phrase "all my relations/relatives" in prayer and ceremony.[38] This phrase encompasses all of the created order, not only human relatives. This relatedness is also highlighted in the way animals are often spoken of as "the four-legged," while we are "the two-legged." The phrase moves further into the created order: "Even what biologists describe as inanimate, we call our relatives. We can understand the power of Christ's statement that the stones would cry out."[39]

---

commentators. See Brueggemann, *Genesis*, 40; Mathews, *Genesis*, 187; McKeown, *Genesis*, 30.

35. Brett, "Earthing the Human In Genesis 1–3," 82.

36. Koehler and Baumgartner, "*tôlēdôt*," 1700.

37. Smith, *Decolonizing Methodologies*," 149.

38. For example, this phrase in the land of Mik'ma'ki in which I currently reside is Msit No'kmaq (*Mm-sit Noh-goh-mah*) and is "one of the most meaningful phrases in the language." See *Mi'kmaw Culture-Spirituality*.

39. McKay, "An Aboriginal Christian Perspective on the Integrity of Creation," 53.

The inter-relatedness is also frequently recognized by Indigenous peoples in the sacramental understanding of eating. To quote at length Kidwell, Noley, and Tinker:

> Corn and all food stuffs are our relatives, just as much as those who live in adjacent lodges . . . Thus, eating is sacramental, to use a euro–theological word, because we are eating our relatives. Not only are we related to corn, beans, and squash . . . but even those other relatives like Buffalo, Deer, Squirrel and Fish ultimately gain their strength and growth because they too eat of the plenty provided by the Mother—eating grasses, leaves, nuts, and algae that also grow out of the Mother's bosom. When we eat, we understand that we are benefiting from the lives that have gone before us, that all our human ancestors have also returned to the earth and have become part of what nourishes us today. Thus, one can never eat without remembering the gift of the Mother, of all our relatives in this world, and of all those who have gone before us.[40]

Indigenous ways of knowing is built upon relationality and permeates life, belief, and practice. Relational language is used to describe the interconnected and interdependent nature of life in the community of creation. While people of other nations may not use or feel comfortable with this type of worldview and language, Indigenous followers of Jesus find deep resonance with their cultural teachings and the Scriptures on this matter.

The Relational Triangle

Given what has been argued above, a helpful way to understand humanity's relationship with creation and Creator is as a relational triangle. This triangulation of reciprocal relationship is established in the creation narrative. To support this type of conception as an appropriate theological model, support from the wider witness of Scripture will be utilized (see figure 1 by the author):

---

40. Kidwell, Noley, and Tinker, *A Native American Theology*, 81. While the language and approach is different, the ultimate importance and sacramental nature of eating is also argued in Wirzba, *Food and Faith*.

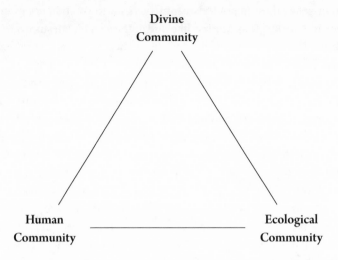

Community of Creation

As a triangulation, the relationships represented are often triangular, i.e. affecting and connecting and affecting all three points together. But the nature of the triangular relationship also shows that the sides of the triangle, as it were, indicate a continual relationship between two points uniquely as well. In other words, there is evidence of good and bad relations between two different points of the triangle in the Scriptures.

God and non-Human Creation

The seven-day creation narrative portrays a clear relationship between Creator and non-human creation. The land obeys the command of Creator in Genesis 1 and produces plant life. In Gen 1:22 aquatic life and birdlife are commanded to be fruitful and multiply just as humanity is. The language is clearly reciprocal: God commands that they do something (be fruitful and multiply), this is their response to his gracious gift—but the very command is at the same time called a blessing. In the act of procreation, all life simultaneously delights in the grace-gift of God and reciprocates the gift with ongoing obedience and co-creative activities.

The continual relationship between God and the ecological community is drawn upon by Jesus in Matt 6:28–29: "Observe the lilies of the field, how they grow: they do not toil or spin, but I say to you that not even Solomon in all his glory was dressed like one of these." Here, Jesus draws upon the observed continual gift of life and sustenance from Creator. Perhaps the most theologically dense expression of the continued relationship between Creator and non-human creation is Psalm 104. After a description of the act of creation in vv. 5–9, Psalm 104 next moves in vv. 10–13 to describe "a portrayal of God's continuing creativity and lavish care of the earth that he has made."[41] In vv. 14–23 the grace-framed relationship becomes even clearer, as God's gift is described as superabundance—the earth has more water than it needs, creatures have more than enough food, and wine provides not just satiation but gladness. In short, "The bounty of God, the outpouring of his goodness and plenty, go beyond what is essential to maintain life."[42] The psalm goes on to talk about mountains, trees, and a variety of animals, all of which are described as valuable in and of themselves. So too does the created sun, moon, day and night, serve other parts of the community of creation. The night is in service to the animals that hunt at night, and the day serves humans to hunt by the sun's light (vv. 19–23). The psalm moves to speak of great sea creatures in vv. 25–26,[43] and then focuses once again on the gracious gift of Creator:

> All your creations wait for you to give them their food on time. When you give it to them, they gather it up; when you open your hand, they are filled completely full! But when you hide your face, they are terrified; when you take away their breath, they die and return to dust. When you let loose your breath, they are created, and you make the surface of the ground brand-new again. (Ps 104:27–30, CEB)

The psalm ends the way many psalms end, with praise and thanksgiving. In the face of such a superlative gift, God is offered back praise. But the praise of God as an act of thankfulness and reciprocity for gifts is not confined to humanity alone. Psalm 104 hopes that the LORD will find joy in what he has made (v. 31) and hopes that God will find pleasing the praise of the psalmist. Other psalms say that the heavens tell the glory of God (Ps 19:2), the heavens declare his righteousness (Ps 50:6; 97:6), the heavens

41. Harrelson, "On God's Care for the Earth: Psalm 104," 20.

42. Ibid.

43. Ps 104:26 may be better translated as "Leviathan that you formed to play with." This would further indicate the relationship and pleasure God takes in his creation. Compare Job 41:1–5.

praise his wonderful deed, and the entire psalter concludes with the call: "let every living thing praise the LORD" (Ps 150:6). Furthermore, Psalm 103 just prior ends with a call for all of creation to bless the Lord: "All you heavenly forces, bless the LORD . . . All God's creatures, bless the LORD! Everywhere, throughout his kingdom, let my whole being bless the LORD! (Ps 103:21–22). This arrangement perhaps suggests that Psalm 104 is in some sense the response to this call at the end of Psalm 103, showing how many different created things do the work of blessing the LORD.[44]

Finally, Psalm 104 ends on a jarring note: "Let sinners be wiped clean from the earth; let the wicked be no more." Why would such a magisterial psalm end on such a serious note? Sin does not fit the cycle of reciprocity within the triangular relationship of which humanity is a part. To break this circle of reciprocity is to bring disequilibrium and imbalance. Sin affects the web of relationships humanity is in, and so the psalmist calls for the removal of the sinner, with the phrase "perish from the earth" being unique within the psalter. Jeremiah 12:4 also recognizes the interconnectedness, seeing the evils of the people devastating the non-human creation.

Another significant passage that speaks to the ongoing relationship between Creator and non-human creation is God's response to Job in chapters 38–41. God's response provides a creational collage, reflecting what William Brown calls "the full self-revelation of creation, and it is a wonder to behold."[45] Through the variety of descriptions of the ordered world and fellow creatures, Job and the reader are shown that the world and its wild inhabitants are not dependent upon humanity. God's long response to Job makes it clear that he continues to have a relationship with non-human creation which humanity has no part in.[46] This perspective limits what it means to be God's image bearer who is called to rule and subdue creation (more on this below). It ought to also cause us to find more inclusive ways of doing theology.[47] Indeed, in the book of Job readers are encouraged to seek wisdom from non-human creation: "ask Behemoth, and he will teach

44. The call to "bless" the Creator is a revealing word to use in the context of our discussion as well. Whereas the praise of God is to admire and extol his deeds and character, to bless God, the ultimate source of all things, is to offer as best as possible some sort of reciprocal blessing to him.

45. Brown, "Wisdom and the Art of Inhabitance," 10.

46. Ibid., states "In YHWH's answer, Job is privileged to behold creation at its most wondrous and terrifying, while discovering that he is not centrally or hierarchically related to any of it."

47. Balabanski, "Critiquing Anthropocentric Cosmology," 152.

you, the birds in the sky, and they will tell you; or talk to earth, and it will teach you; the fish of the sea will recount it for you" (Job 12:7–10). This statement, in the heart of the wisdom literature of the Scriptures, makes a profound statement about sourcing out wisdom. Wisdom and the fear of God is not knowledge exclusive to the human community but can be found in the wider community of creation. The Earth Bible's third ecojustice principle is the Principle of Voice: "Earth is a living entity capable of raising its voice in celebration and against injustice."[48]

It is clear from the above evidence that God cares for non-human creation directly and apart from humanity. But this relationship is not simply one of care over an object, nor is it simply delight over something made, like a painter enjoying art on a canvas. The care is relational. This can be stated confidently because the Scriptures also indicate God's displeasure at times with aspect of non-human creation, and God delivering consequences upon non-human creation. Two examples in Scripture show this to be the case. The first example is the covenant God creates in Gen 9:5 after the flood. The Common English Bible rightly subtitles this as "God's covenant with all life,"[49] while many modern English translations provide a more anthropocentric subtitle like "God's Covenant with Noah" (NIV) or "The Covenant with Noah" (NRSV). Not only is the covenant with all the living creatures, but God also makes it clear that animals are held accountable for impermissible shedding of blood. God's reciprocal relationship with non-human creation is ongoing and he has expectations of the ecological community. Exodus 21:28 continues to hold up this law from Genesis 9, with an ox that kills a person being put to death for its action.

Another example of non-human creation being held accountable for improper action is Ezekiel 6. In this chapter God condemns both the people and the mountains for allowing the pollution of idolatry: "For Ezekiel, the mountains are . . . harborers of other gods that are in league with the people who commit crimes against Yahweh, implying that they have a moral condition and that they are guilty by their association with the Israelites."[50] Ezekiel views the people and the land as intimately connect-

48. The principles are printed in each of the Earth Bible volumes and can be found online here: www.webofcreation.org/Earthbible/ebprinciples.html. Details on the Earth Bible project can be found at www.webofcreation.org/earth-bible.

49. The New King James Version also properly sub-titles the section as "God's Covenant with Creation."

50. Briggs, "Idols and Land Grabs," 48.

ed, and both deserving of punishment.[51] Yet, in this condemnation, God is said to be "crushed" or "broken" in Ezek 6:9, a striking metaphorical picture that indicates brokenness of spirit.[52] The example from Ezekiel not only highlights the ongoing relationship between God and non-human creation, but also provides a clear example of the relational triangle: "God is so entwined with the relational web of the world that everything that happens in creation has an effect on the divine realm."[53] Sin brings about disharmony throughout the triangulation.

Humanity and non-Human Creation

The previous example from Ezekiel 6 illustrates this side of the triangle as well. The acts of people which grieve the Creator inevitably come to bear on the land too—the land suffers from the disequilibrium humanity brings into the community of creation. Israel's dishonoring of the Creator is at the same time a dishonoring of the land they occupy and inevitably drags the land into the brokenness of the relationship.

In the creation narrative a deep connection between the human community and the ecological community forms. The intimate relationship between humanity and the Creator looks like a lush green forest garden.[54] A tree represents God's gift of life. In that setting this part of the triangle is clearly expressed as a reciprocal relationship: the land provides the food in Gen 1:29–31 and then God establishes how humanity will give back to the land in reciprocity, by serving and conforming to the garden (see the discussion above on Gen 2:15).

A potential objection to reading this connection between the land and humanity in a relational manner might be that God always prioritizes humanity as the crown jewel of creation because it alone is the part of creation capable of being in a relationship with God. Yet, at several points it is clear in the Scriptures that God does in fact act against humanity in deference to the land. We have already encountered an example in Ezekiel 6 of a part of the land bearing the consequences of idolatry. Another example comes in Leviticus 18, which is a chapter on unlawful sexual relations. God says through Moses:

51. Briggs, "Idols and Land Grabs," 49.
52. Koehler and Baumgartner, "šbr," 1403–4.
53. Briggs, "Idols and Land Grabs," 49
54. Newsom, "Common Ground," 64–65.

> Do not make yourselves unclean in any of these ways because that
> is how the nations that I am throwing out before you became un-
> clean. That is also how the land became unclean, and I held it liable
> for punishment, and the land vomited out its inhabitants. But all
> of you must keep my rules and my regulations. You must not do
> any of these detestable things, neither citizen nor immigrant who
> lives with you because the people who had the land before you
> did all of these detestable things and the land became unclean,
> so that the land does not vomit you out because you have made
> it unclean, just as it vomited out the nations that were before you
> (Lev 18:24–28, CEB).

This is a remarkable passage that confirms the triangular relationship.
Like Ezekiel 6, the land, tied to humanity, bears the punishment that the
humans face. But the passage next goes on to show the land itself acting in
retaliation, with the very descriptive act of peoples being vomited out. In this
passage, God declares that the Canaanites sinned against the land, and the
Israelite conquest was both God and the land's ejection of the people. This
same type of punishment is not exclusive to non-Israelites, as Israel will also
be punished for sinning against the land at the end of 2 Chronicles:

> The Babylonians burned God's temple down, demolished the walls
> of Jerusalem, and set fire to all its palaces, destroying everything
> of value. Finally, he exiled to Babylon anyone who survived the
> killing so that they could be his slaves and the slaves of his children
> until Persia came to power. This is how the LORD's word spoken
> by Jeremiah was carried out. *The land finally enjoyed its sabbath
> rest.* For as long as it lay empty, it rested, until seventy years were
> completed. (2 Chr 36:17–21, CEB).

This passage is an important example of God prioritizing the needs of
the land over the people.[55] The exile of the Jewish people and the terrible
destruction brought by the Babylonians are in part because they did not
honor the land's need for rest. The sabbath rest spoken of here points to
one of the most important components of the Mosaic law when discussing
the relationship with the land. God reminds the Israelites in the Law that
the land belongs to him and is given as a gift (Exod 6:8; Lev 25:23). The law
sought to remind Israel of this fact through the rhythm of sabbath. Not only
were the Israelites to establish the weekly pattern of resting every seventh

---

55. In reflecting on a Keetoowah creation story, Woodley states that one of its teachings is the same as what I have described here: "when humans have broken harmony with
creation, they have broken harmony with the Creator" (Woodley, "Early Dialogue," 97).

day just as Creator did, but they are told to honor a sabbatical year in which debts were forgiven, indentured slaves were released, and the land was left to grow fallow. The language in Leviticus 25 is very clearly relational language reflecting this triangular relationship:

> Six years you shall sow your field, and six years you shall prune your vineyard, and you shall gather its yield. But in the seventh year it shall be a Sabbath of complete rest *for the land*—a Sabbath *for Yahweh*; you must not sow your field, and you must not prune your vineyard. You must not reap your harvest's aftergrowth, and you must not harvest the grapes of your unpruned vines—it shall be a year of complete rest *for the land*. (Lev 25:3–6, LEB)

This section goes on to talk about everyone and anyone, human and animal alike, being allowed to eat whatever the land chooses to provide during that year, but it cannot be tilled or harvested. The passage indicates that there is rest for all parties within the triangulation. This passage shows us that a lack of reciprocity with the land by the Israelites meant that God steps in and prioritizes the need of the land. "The exile of the people from the land allowed the land to remain fallow and finally enjoy the Sabbaths that had been commanded through Moses."[56] This perspective is echoed also in Lev 26:34:

> At that time, while it is devastated and you are in enemy territory, the land will enjoy its sabbaths, as opposed to continuous production. At that time, the land will rest and enjoy its sabbaths. During the whole time it is devastated, it will have the rest it didn't have during the sabbaths you lived in it. (CEB)

After the return from the Babylonian exile, the Israelites recognize the error of their ways and pledge to give the land its rest in Neh 10:31: "Every seventh year we won't plant crops, and we will return anything held in debt."

The final point of interest in the sabbatical year laws is the recognition of the human community's dependence on the land. Even in the midst of letting the land grow fallow, providing rest for Yahweh, for the land, and for themselves—even then the land graciously provides: "whatever the land produces during its sabbath will be your food" (Lev 25:6). God also states that he will send an extra blessing in the sixth year for provisions in the sabbatical year. This puts humans in their place: we are dependent on the

---

56. Boda, *1–2 Chronicles*, 427.

gifts provided by the Creator and mother earth, the land takes care of us. This is a grace-gift. The land, as is often the case, is the median place for the blessings received from the Creator.

God acting against humanity in defense of the land is not confined to the Sabbath. In the primordial flood stories, the land is an essential element in the story mentioned numerous times—primarily identified as ʾereṣ, though ʾădāmâ is used occasionally as well. The primary source of God's grief is because of humanity: "The LORD saw that humanity had become thoroughly evil on the earth and that every idea their minds thought up was always completely evil (Gen 6:5). The corruption of humanity is great "upon the earth" (Gen 6:5) and God grieves that he made humankind "on the earth" (6:6). The result of this grief is God's declaration that he will wipe humankind "from upon the face of the earth" (6:7). God works to return the harmony of ṭôb (good) by removing the disharmony of rāʿâ (evil). God's flood judgment is not simply to punish humanity, but to also remove the corrupting influence from the land—the flood is not just a cleansing *from* the earth, but also a cleansing *for* the earth (Gen 6:17).[57] It is at this point that the description of the judgment expands "to animals, to creeping things, and to the birds of heaven, for a I regret that I have made them" (6:7). The relational triangle is on display here: the disobedience of humanity in Genesis 3 has worked its corruptive influence elsewhere in the community of creation, and disharmony has now corrupted the circle of relationship among God, humanity, and non-human creation. While a covenant will not be mentioned until God is speaking to Noah in Gen 6:18, God's declaration in 6:7 provides the framework for why the postflood Covenant is with all of creation (9:10, 15–17), as they are the living things judged in the flood.[58]

But what type of corruptive influence might humanity have had with fellow created kin such that they too are deserving of punishment? It is at this point that one needs to recall the inter-dependence established in the creation narrative. It is precisely the creatures who are placed into a reciprocal relationship with the land in Gen 1:30 who are named for destruction

57. Recall earlier that God has defended the land from humanity's corrupting influence, both the Canaanites and the Israelites. This work to cleanse the promised land is the same work of the flood, but on a smaller scale and without the use of flood waters, as God has promised to no longer cleanse by means of a flood (Gen 9:11).

58. John Olley notes that readers might be forgiven for expecting the covenant to only be with Noah and his family given Gen 6:18. See Olley, "Mixed Blessings For Animals," 130.

in 6:7. Aquatic life, equally created by God, are not placed into an inter-dependent relationship with the land the way humanity, animal life, buglife, and birdlife are in the text. If the nature of this gift of food is to establish inter-dependence and reciprocity towards mother earth, then perhaps this provides a glimpse into the corrupting nature of humanity's rebellion with our fellow creatures. Adam and Eve's progeny have forsaken their responsibility to serve and conform to the land (Gen 2:15), and as God's imagers who are charged with ruling and subduing as a first among their created kin,[59] the abdication of their responsibilities to the land corrupts fellow created kin who were also placed into an inter-dependent relationship with the land, pollutes the land such that it needs defending by God, and grieves the very heart of the Creator: "the 'sorry' of God is the deep hurt God feels because of a deep hurt in the Earth."[60]

God and Humanity

The final side of the relational triangle is the connection between God and humanity. This vertical relationship with God is the subject of the majority of the Scriptures and does not require focus here. But there are several important points within this vertical relationship between humanity and God that pertains to land.

The land is given as a gift to all of its inhabitants, of whom we are just one. But it is also important to recognize that God's design was for humanity to be a gift to creation as well.[61] Our foundational text for a biblical anthropology is Gen 1:26–27 and its declaration that humanity is made in the

---

59. I use this language deliberately, not only to remind one of our common creatureliness, but because it serves to remind the reader of the kind of kingly rule of which God approves. To quote Bauckham: "Since Genesis 1 presents this authority as a kind of kingly rule, it is relevant to recall the only kind of human rule over other humans that the Old Testament approves. The book of Deuteronomy allows Israel to have a king of sorts, but it interprets this kingship in a way designed to subvert all ordinary notions of rule (17:14–20). If Israel must have a king, then the king must be a brother. He is a brother set over his brothers and sisters, but still a brother, and forbidden any of the ways in which rulers exalt themselves over and entrench their power over their subjects. His rule becomes tyranny the moment he forgets that the horizontal relationship of brother/sisterhood is primary, kingship secondary" (Bauckham, *Living with Other Creatures*, 5). Iain Provan makes a similar point that in the Scriptures kingship is always within kinship, see Provan, *Seriously Dangerous Religion*, 225–26.

60. Fejo, "The Voice of the Earth," 2:142.

61. As mentioned above, it was first not good for the land to be alone in Genesis 2.

image of God. Despite the breakdown of relationship and consequences in the garden in Genesis 3, humanity is still in the image, a fact readers are reminded of in Gen 5:1–2: "On the day God created humanity, he made them in the likeness God and created them male and female. He blessed them and called them humanity on the day they were created" (CEB). Theological discussion on the *Imago Dei* normally focuses on human abilities or characteristics (like intelligence, self-awareness, etc). But to be an imager, or to be a representative, for God on earth is not primarily about what characteristics makes us human.[62] It has to do with the call and responsibility as human beings to represent the Creator on the earth: "people are delegated a godlike role (function) in the world where he places them."[63] Being in the image of God is about the responsibility mandated and a status held.[64] The superabundant gift of life, dwelling, and food is provided by God and the land. This initiates grace-framed reciprocity. And as was discussed above, the Creator describes what humanity's ongoing reciprocal response to the grace-gift should be. Immediately after the declaration that humanity is in the image of God comes the creation mandate or cultural mandate: "Be fruitful and multiply, and fill the earth and subdue it, and rule over the fish of the sea and the birds of heaven, and over every animal that moves upon the earth" (Gen 1:28, LEB). As many know, this verse was made notorious by Lynn White's 1967 article "The Historical Roots of Our Ecologic Crisis," pinning the blame, not entirely without merit, for our current ecological crisis on the Judeo-Christian reception of this verse.[65] This four-page article has been hugely influential for some good reason, but also contains some serious flaws, only one of which I want to address here for our discussion.[66] Within the triangulation of the grace-framed relationship, the vocation of human beings to be God's imagers would be to not just imitate the creativity of God that has already been witnessed in the days of creation, but *to actively aid creation in reciprocating its relationship to the Creator.* Understanding this helps to properly live out what it means

62. I would suggest that those human characteristics frequently discussed as being in the "image of God" are more accurately those things that describe us in the likeness (*dĕmût*) of God (Gen 1:26).

63. Walton, *Lost World of Genesis*, 67.

64. Michael Heiser states: "It is what we are by definition. The image is not an ability we have, but a status. We are God's representatives on earth. To be human is to image God," in Heiser, *The Unseen Realm*, 42–43.

65. White, "The Historical Roots of Our Ecologic Crisis," 1203–7.

66. For a fuller critique, see Bauckham, *Living with Other Creatures*, 14–62.

for humanity to subdue the earth.[67] This seems to be abundantly clear in the very next sentence, "Take charge of the fish of the sea, the birds in the sky, and everything crawling on the ground" (Gen 1:28, CEB). Recall that the Creator, whom humanity now represents, has already given a mandate to the fish and the birds in v. 22, "Be fertile and multiply and fill the waters in the seas, and let the birds multiply on the earth" (CEB). The mandate to God's imagers to take charge over wildlife is expressly to help them flourish and thereby obey Creator's command. To do this, we listen and learn from the Creator, the land, and the animals themselves, as they are the ones who received the command.[68] This charge to subdue the earth is also immediately curtailed by God, announcing that the plants that were co-created by God and the land in 1:9–12 are now given to many creatures as food. This firmly restricts the creation mandate to subdue and rule, as God makes it clear that food is not theirs to go and subdue for themselves, it is a gift given to them and others, and is supported by "brother sun" and "sister moon," who's job is to rule (*memšālâ*) the day and night, in part to assist creatures to find food (Ps 104:19–23).

When the relationship between God and humanity is fractured, there is a response from the land. The best example of this is the result of the rebellion in the garden. Our first parents disregard God's one rule in Genesis 3. The result is removal from the beauty of the garden, which removes access from the tree of life. This results in difficulty in labor for the woman and a potentially fractious relationship between the partners. But it also means that the reciprocal relationship with the land has now grown more difficult. What was to be graceful reciprocity will now at times be begrudging reciprocity. Because of this triangulation, humanity's relational tie to the earth means that our sins affect the entire web of relationships in the community of creation. And the land will punish humanity for our rebellion too, as now "weeds and thistles will grow for you, even as you eat the field's plants; by the sweat of your face you will eat bread" (Gen 3:18–19, CEB).

Finally, the example of Noah shows how a right relationship with God will positively affect the community of creation. The prelude to Noah's story

67. The word subdue has so often been envisioned as if we were talking about Dwayne 'The Rock' Johnson placing a fellow wrestler in a stranglehold until they tap out. The image we should draw to mind instead is one of a bee-keeper, in which, if we don't respect and give space for their work, we will get stung.

68. Discussion of our environmental "stewardship" has too often been built upon the hubristic assumption that we know what is best for the non-human creation around us.

established God's appraisal of the wickedness on the earth and His impending judgment to cleanse the earth. But immediately after the pronouncement of judgment in Gen 6:7, the reader is surprised by one who, in the midst of the evil upon the earth, has found favor in God's eyes (Gen 6:8–9). It is only Noah who is exemplary amongst his generation (Gen 6:9), and yet his right relationship will result in not only the safety of his family, but also of representatives from amongst the animals. Righteous Noah is fulfilling the mandate that God gave in the creation narrative.

Conclusions

From the above exegetical work, I would like to draw a number of conclusions, connect some current Indigenous spiritual practices with the text, and draw some lines of connection with my fellow authors who have articulated theologies of land. First, when the language of 'creation care' continues to be used, a false narrative perpetuates the belief that humanity provides some sort of essential service for non-human creation. In doing so, the creation is often objectified and de-sacralized. I have tried to show from the Scriptures that this is simply not the case. An intercultural reading of the text brings about the shedding of an anthropocentric hermeneutic and ought to bring about the reformation of how we speak about our relationship to creation, "human beings are part of a whole, not lords over that whole but ethically responsible to it."[69] We as the human community are the needy ones—the land takes care of us. As Kimmerer has stated, part of our restoration with Creator and creation is "re-story-ation." In Indigenous ways of knowing, humanity is not only within the community creation instead of hierarchically above it, but are "often referred to as 'the younger brothers of Creation.' We say that humans have the least experience with how to live and thus the most to learn—we must look to our teachers among the other species for guidance."[70] Flowing from a change in perspective and change of how we speak about creation and our relationship to it, we recognize that our actions ought to be tangible expressions of gratefulness toward non-human creation in the lands we inhabit, tangible expressions of reciprocity toward non-human creation, and tangible expressions which promote the flourishing of non-human creation. In these ways we recognize ourselves as part of the community of creation, and we acknowledge both our utter

69. Yeo, "Christ and the Earth In Pauline and Native American Understandings," 203.

70. Kimmerer, *Braiding Sweetgrass*, 9.

dependence on mother earth and our catalytic role, for good and ill, in the community of creation.[71]

Second, Creator placed humanity into and interconnected, interdependent, and harmonious community. From this cosmic and primordial creation story we read that our first parents were placed in a specific location in which they were to live a life of reciprocity with the land and in fellowship with God. From this story we can see that we too have been placed into specific locations and territories in which we are to live lives of reciprocity within the community of creation and in fellowship with God. The effort to universalize theologies of land often derives, knowingly or unknowingly, from a colonial western perspective. This universalizing tendency ignores our creation story of placement within a specific locality and may derive from theologians who themselves do not feel a deep and essential—i.e. Indigenized—connection to the land in which they live and are sustained. As Oscar García-Johnson has noted, the success of European conquest has contributed to this continued landless anthropology and universalizing theology of land. In contrast, Indigenous peoples have always had a strong connection to the land because of this locative understanding of who they are as a people. The land does not belong to them, they belong to the land and they have a spiritual responsibility towards it: "becoming indigenous to a place means living as if your children's future mattered, to take care of the land as if our lives, both material and spiritual, depended on it."[72] As such, their spirituality is a land-based spirituality. Churches that originate from European colonial history have not indigenized, in that they have not connected their spiritual practices to the land in which they reside and are upheld. They have kept their worship and practices landless. Chief Lawrence Hart states:

> when non-Native Christians gather for church in Chicago, Seattle, or Toronto, they typically don't acknowledge the land on which they gather. By words or physical action, they do not attempt to recognize or connect with the very place on which they are privileged to gather. The liturgy or worship service is "placeless"—not

---

71. As the imagers of God, humanity has both the most creative power and the most destructive power in the created order. Provan opens his chapter with this quote from Henry David Thoreau: "Thank God men cannot fly, and lay waste the sky as well as the earth! Journal XIV: August 1, 1860—November 3, 1861." The entry is for January 3, 1861, and can be read at www.walden.org. See Provan, *Seriously Dangerous Religion*, 221.

72. Kimmerer, *Braiding Sweetgrass*, 9.

"placed" in Toronto or "placed" in Seattle. But indigenous peoples typically do "place" their worship.[73]

Second, because of the deep connection to land, which is part of every human being's spiritual DNA, the lack of placement and connection within the community of creation, in a particular location, results in spiritual hollowness. Indigenous peoples have more than most felt the spiritual devastation that comes from displacement as they were forced from their ancestral territories. As one Indigenous elder stated:

> being an Indian means saying that the land is an old friend that your father knew, your grandfather knew—your people have always known. If the land is destroyed, then we too are destroyed. If you people ever take our land, you will be taking our life.[74]

One of the contributing factors to these despicable injustices was the colonizers perspective of land as commodity and object for human exploitation, the very perspective cited in Lynn White's famous article for the roots of the ecological crisis.[75] As García-Johnson has ably discussed, this has meant the commodification not only of the "New World" but also of all the community of creation that resided in those lands.

Finally, the creation stories and the Sabbath laws in the Torah make it clear that the land belongs to the Creator. While almost no believer denies this point, it is in practice denied as recourse to the Doctrine of Discovery or European law on land ownership is the norm. Yet, it is well known that when Columbus was found lost on the shores of Turtle Island, he and many other later Europeans were welcomed and the land and its resources were shared. There was no concept of property ownership amongst the First Nations. This understanding that the land belonged to Creator undergirded the Two Row Wampum treaty as well as agreements like the Peace and Friendship Treaties in Atlantic Canada.[76] In these covenants, the land was to be shared in respect of one another.[77] In reality, the Doctrine of Discovery

73. Hart, "The Earth Is a Song Made Visible," 155–56.

74. Weaver, "Revelation and Epistemology," 30. Here Weaver is quoting Richard Nerysoo, a Gwich'in leader from the North West Territories of Canada.

75. White, "The Historical Roots of Our Ecologic Crisis."

76. For the Two Row Wampum, see www.onondaganation.org/culture/wampum/two-row-wampum-belt-guswenta/. For the Peace and Friendship Treaties, see https://novascotia.ca/archives/mikmaq/results.asp?Search=AR5&SearchList1=all&TABLE2=on.

77. Because of the continued colonization and dispossessing of land, the colonial language of land 'title' and 'ownership' are now frequently used when discussing Indigenous

and colonialism continued to drive European settlers, rather than honoring these covenants. While we continue to live in nation-states which hold to the concept of individual and corporate land ownership, our theological convictions, borne as they are from the biblical text, ought to shape our positions and opinions on matters of immigration and displacement. Not only is personal and corporate land ownership contrary to our theology, but part of what it means to be human is to be placed within a reciprocal relationship to a land. Displacement and the lack of place to call home hampers what it means to be made in God's image. This awareness that Creator has designed humans to be connected to a land caused First Nations to welcome European settlers. Connecting people to a place, whether displaced or immigrant, helps one to be more fully human.

Further Readings

Bauckham, Richard. *Living with Other Creatures: Green Exegesis and Theology*. Waco, TX: Baylor University Press, 2011.
Charleston, Steven, and Elaine A. Robinson, eds. *Coming Full Circle: Constructing Native Christian Theology*. Minneapolis: Fortress, 2015.
Habel Norman C., edited. *The Earth Bible*. 5 vols. Sheffield: Sheffield Academic, 2000–2002.
Journal of NAIITS. 2003–present.
Twiss, Richard. *Rescuing the Gospel from the Cowboys: A Native American Expression of the Jesus Way*. Downers Grove, IL: InterVarsity, 2015.
Woodley, Randy. *Shalom and The Community of Creation: An Indigenous Vision*. Grand Rapids: Eerdmans, 2012.

Bibliography

Alter, Robert. *Genesis*. New York: Norton, 1996.
———. *The Five Books of Moses: A Translation with Commentary*. New York: Norton, 2004.
Balabanski, Vicky. "Critiquing Anthropocentric Cosmology: Retrieving a Stoic 'Permeation Cosmology' in Colossians 1:15–20." In *Exploring Ecological Hermeneutics*, edited by Peter L. Trudinger and Norman C. Habel, 151–60. Society of Biblical Literature Symposium Series. Atlanta: SBL, 2008.
Barclay, John M. G. *Paul and the Gift*. Grand Rapids: Eerdmans, 2015.
Bauckham, Richard. *Bible and Ecology: Rediscovering the Community of Creation*. Waco, TX: Baylor University Press, 2010.

---

land and sovereignty. The numbered treaties that govern most of Canada involved the ceding of land, removing the Indigenous peoples from the bulk of their territory and giving the title to the government.

————. *Living with Other Creatures: Green Exegesis and Theology*. Waco, TX: Baylor University Press, 2011.

Boda, Mark J. *1–2 Chronicles*. Cornerstone Biblical Commentary 5a. Carol Stream, IL: Tyndale House, 2005.

Brett, Mark G. "Earthing The Human In Genesis 1–3." In *Earth Story in Genesis*, edited by Norman C. Habel and Shirley Wurst, 73–86. The Earth Bible 2. Sheffield: Sheffield Academic, 2000.

Brett, Mark G., and Daniel Zacharias. "To Serve Her and Be Conformed to Her: An Intercultural Conversation on Gen 2:15." Forthcoming.

Briggs, William. "Idols and Land Grabs, Ancient and Modern: Creation and Ecotheology in Ezekiel 6; 35:1—36:15." *Horizons in Biblical Theology* 40/1 (2018) 41–64.

Brown, William P. "Wisdom and the Art of Inhabitance." Paper presented at the Annual Meeting of the Institute for Biblical Research. Denver, 2018.

Brueggemann, Walter. *Genesis*. Interpretation. Atlanta: John Knox, 1982.

Fejo, Wali. "The Voice of the Earth: An Indigenous Reading of Genesis 9." In *Earth Story in Genesis*. eds. Norman C. Habel and Shirley Wurst, 140–46. The Earth Bible 2. Sheffield: Sheffield Academic, 2000.

Fretheim, Terence E. "Creator, Creature, And Co-Creation in Genesis 1–2." In *All Things New: Essays in Honor of Roy A. Harrisville*, edited by Arland J. Hultgren, Donald H. Juel, and Jack Dean Kingsbury, 1:11–20. St. Paul: Word & World, 1992.

Habel, Norman C. "Geophany: The Earth Story in Genesis 1." In *Earth Story in Genesis*, 34–48. The Earth Bible 2. Sheffield: Sheffield Academic, 2000.

Harrelson, Walter J. "On God's Care for the Earth: Psalm 104." *Currents in Theology and Mission* 2/1 (1975) 19–22.

Hart, Lawrence. "The Earth Is a Song Made Visible: A Cheyenne Christian Perspective." In *Buffalo Shout, Salmon Cry: Conversations on Creation, Land Justice, and Life Together*, edited by Steve Heinrichs, 153–61. Harrisonburg, VT: Herald, 2013.

Heinrichs, Steve, ed. *Buffalo Shout, Salmon Cry: Conversations On Creation, Land Justice, And Life Together*. Harrisonburg, VT: Herald, 2013.

Heiser, Michael S. *The Unseen Realm: Recovering the Supernatural Worldview of the Bible*. Bellingham, WA: Lexham, 2015.

Jenni, Ernst, and Claus Westermann, eds. *Theological Lexicon of the Old Testament*. 3 vols. Translated by Mark E. Biddle. Peabody, MA: Hendrickson, 1997.

Kidwell, Clara Sue, Homer Noley, and George E. "Tink" Tinker. *A Native American Theology*. Maryknoll, NY: Orbis, 2001.

Koehler, Ludwig, and Walter Baumgartner. *The Hebrew and Aramaic Lexicon of the Old Testament*. Translated by M. E. J. Richardson. 5 vols. Leiden: Brill, 2000.

Martin, Oren R. *Bound for the Promised Land: The Land Promise in God's Redemptive Plan*. Downers Grove, IL: InterVarsity, 2015.

Mathews, Kenneth A. *Genesis 1—11:26*. New American Commentary 1A. Nashville: Broadman & Holman, 1995.

McKeown, James. *Genesis*. Two Horizons Old Testament Commentary. Grand Rapids: Eerdmans, 2008.

Moltmann, Jürgen. *God in Creation: A New Theology of Creation and the Spirit of God*. The Gifford Lectures. San Francisco: Harper & Row, 1985.

Moo, Douglas J., and Jonathan A. Moo. *Creation Care: A Biblical Theology of the Natural World*. Grand Rapids: Zondervan, 2018.

Newsom, Carol A. "Common Ground: An Ecological Reading of Genesis 2–3." In *Earth Story in Genesis*, edited by Norman C. Habel and Shirley Wurst, 60–72. The Earth Bible 2. Sheffield: Sheffield Academic, 2000.

Olley, John W. "Mixed Blessings for Animals: The Contrasts of Genesis 9." In *Earth Story in Genesis*, edited by Norman C. Habel and Shirley Wurst, 130–39. The Earth Bible 2. Sheffield: Sheffield Academic, 2000.

Provan, Iain W. *Seriously Dangerous Religion: What the Old Testament Really Says and Why It Matters*. Waco, TX: Baylor University Press, 2014.

Smith, Linda Tuhiwai. *Decolonizing Methodologies: Research and Indigenous Peoples*. 2nd ed. London: Zed, 2013.

Wallace, Howard N. "Rest for the Earth?: Another Look at Genesis 2.1–3." In *Earth Story in Genesis*, 49–59. The Earth Bible 2. Sheffield: Sheffield Academic, 2000.

Walton, John H. *Genesis*. NIV Application Commentary. Grand Rapids: Zondervan, 2001.

———. *The Lost World of Genesis One: Ancient Cosmology and the Origins Debate*. Downers Grove, IL: InterVarsity Press, 2009.

White, Lynn, Jr. "The Historical Roots of Our Ecologic Crisis." *Science* 155/3767 (1967) 1203–7.

Wirzba, Norman. *Food and Faith: A Theology of Eating*. Cambridge: Cambridge University, 2011.

Woodley, Randy. *Shalom and the Community of Creation: An Indigenous Vision*. Grand Rapids: Eerdmans, 2012.

———. "Early Dialogue in the Community of Creation." In *Buffalo Shout, Salmon Cry: Conversations On Creation, Land Justice, And Life Together*, edited by Steve Heinrichs, 92–103. Harrisonburg, VT: Herald, 2013.

Yeo, K. K. "Christ and the Earth in Pauline and Native American Understandings." In *Cross-Cultural Paul: Journeys to Others, Journeys to Ourselves*, edited by Charles H. Cosgrove, Herold Weiss, and K. K. Yeo, 179–218. Grand Rapids: Eerdmans, 2005.

4

Negotiation and/or Conquest of the Land

Reading the Land of Promise Motif in the
Hexateuch through Decolonial Lenses

Hulisani Ramantswana

Abstract

The Promised Land/Land of Promise motif is an essential component in the context of the Hexateuch. From a decolonial perspective, the Promised Land motif cannot be divorced from the
dynamics of power. The Hexateuch reflects two different perspectives of inheriting the Promised Land: first, inheriting the land
from the position of powerlessness—inheriting the land through
negotiations for space in a space already occupied by others; and
inheriting the land from the position of power militarily through
the use of force. The conquest model, while it is the dominant
ideology within the Hexateuch, it is not the sole ideology; thus,
decolonial alternative also evident in the text although suppressed.

Introduction

I am descendant of the Vhavhirwa people, who settled within the
Vhavenḓa kingdom in mountainous area of Swongozwi, an area that
was one of the royal seats of the Vhavenda kings, the Ramabulana. The
Vhavenḓa kings such as Makhado (c. 1840–1895) and his successor

98

Mphephu (c. 1865–1925) resisted the colonial rule over the Vhavenḓa kingdom. The initial acceptance of the Boers to settle in their territory was a deed representing hospitality of our ancestors not a surrender of land.[1] However, the colonial machinery continued to plough on with the banishment of King Mphephu and the imprisonment of some of the mahosi (chiefs) and by sowing division within the kingdom. It was in this process that the fertile mountain range of our ancestors was forcefully and violently taken as they were pushed to less fertile areas. Notwithstanding the land claims, the Swongozwi area is yet to be returned to its rightful owners. So we wonder for how long our people have to wait as the promise of land remains a dream continually deferred.

The land in Africa remains an emotive issue postliberation of the African states. Politically, the liberation movements could not ignore the land question, as it touched on the nature of the oppression that the African people suffered from European colonialism.[2] The land question is inseparable from the Bible in our (South) African context. As Mosala notes,

> [The Bible] was there at the founding of modern South Africa when white colonisers dispossessed the Africans of their land and created out of them a wage class with nothing but their labour power to sell. When Apartheid, as a specific ideology of racial oppression and exploitation was established, the Bible was there. The Bible is there in the present constitution of the South African government. The Bible is there in every aspect of South African life in curious and often violently contradictory ways.[3]

Thus, the Bible presents both a problem and a solution in dealing with the land issue, particularly so in a context where the masses regard it as a book of faith. With European colonialism, the Bible was part of the colonising instruments, and yet it has become an African book shaping people's faith.

This paper is structured as follows: first, it addresses the issue of land and the Bible in light of the role played by colonialism in the African context; second, it focusses on reconstruction theology, considering the dynamics of freedom and land, and lastly, it gives attention to the motif of the promised land as projected in the Hexateuch.[4]

---

1. See Braun, "The Returns of the King," 276.

2. Mosala, "Land," 41.

3. Mosala, "Land," 41.

4. The Hexateuch is a hermeneutical construct as Genesis–Joshua is part of a larger story, which scholars refer to as the Primary History or the Enneateuch (Genesis–Kings).

Land and the Bible:
Colonial-Apartheid Period and Stolen Land

In the African context, a statement attributed to Jomo Kenyatta captures the dilemma that exists between Africans, the land, the presence of the other, and the Bible: "When Europeans came to Africa, they had the Bible and the African had the land. They gave the Bible to the African and told him to hold it in his hand, close his eyes, and pray. When the African opened his eyes, he had the Bible and the European had his land."[5] The Europeans' deceptive swapping of the land for the Bible was not an innocent process—it was a violent process. As Maluleke notes, "the fact that it [the Bible] was 'used' in conquest will always haunt us even if we pretend otherwise."[6] Now that the African has the Bible in hand, I wonder: Does the African have to pray with eyes wide open or with at most one eye closed, as others forms of exploitation may be ongoing?

The African cannot afford to pray with both eyes closed, given that the land problem in Africa (and wherever modern colonialism has left its footprint) is also founded on the church's racist Doctrine of Discovery pronounced by Pope Nicholas V in 1452 in the Papal bull *Dum Diversas*:

> We grant to you by these present document with our Apostolic authority, full and free permission to invade, search out, capture and subjugate the Saracens and pagans and any other unbelievers and enemies of Christ wherever they may be, as well as their kingdoms, duchies, counties, principalities, lands, towns, villas and other properties . . . and to reduce their persons into perpetual slavery. And appropriate all their kingdoms, commands, retainers, dominance, and any possessions to yourself and to your successors to use and enjoy these assets fully and freely.[7]

This papal bull along with other church pronouncements, as noted in García-Johnson's chapter in this book, ecclesiastically and theologically granted the Europeans the right to take over non-European territories. The Doctrine of Discovery was in effect the church's legitimation of, among other things, first, the racialization of human society, with

---

Beyond that, it is part of a broader canonical story, the Hebrew Bible or Old Testament (see Dozeman, Römer, and Schmid, eds., *Pentateuch, Hexateuch, or Enneateuch*).

5. As quoted from Khapoya, *African Experience*, 103.

6. Maluleke, "Postcolonial Mission," 519

7. As quote from, Adiele, *The Popes*, 313.

Europeans/whites as superior and others as inferior; second, the capture, enslavement and dispossession of the lands and goods of those regarded as inferior and pagans; third, immediate and automatic political power and property rights for the invaders as lands—the so-called "new worlds," which were in fact already inhabited—were colonized without the knowledge or the consent of the native people.[8]

In our African context (and elsewhere), with the rise of colonialism, land-rich people were forcefully transitioned to land-poor people. The colonization of inhabited lands, therefore, should be described for what it was: *theft* or *stealing* of land. The notion of *conquest*, while it explains the colonial process, also gives the false impression of conqueror takes all, as though the game was fair and just. It is proper to speak of *stolen land* in our African context. The 1884 Berlin conference, at which the colonial powers partitioned Africa, with each getting a piece of the African land, was a curse on African people. Therefore, Adebayo rightly speaks of the "curse of Berlin," which needs to be lifted.[9]

In the South African context, the curse was as follows: In 1913, the colonial government, the Union of South Africa, promulgated the Natives Land Act, which spatially distributed land between whites and blacks as follows: 92 percent of land belonged to whites, whereas just a meager 8 percent of land was set for blacks. Following the Land Act of 1938, the Reserve Land was increased to 13 percent for blacks, with 87 percent of the land belonging to whites. Furthermore, at the heart of the policy of apartheid and separation were the following acts: the Group Areas Act (1950), the Bantu Authorities Act (1951), and the Promotion of Black Self-Government Act (1959), all of which were aimed at separating people on the basis of their language and culture, which in turn necessarily determined who stays where. It is this curse or theft which has yet to be fully reversed in the current post-colonial, post-apartheid South Africa.

In neighbouring Zimbabwe, which attained its independence from the British colonial empire in 1980, freedom did not amount to a speedy return of the land to the indigenous people. After twenty years of slow progress in the land reform process, in 2001 the government, under the leadership of the then president Robert Mugabe, introduced the Fast Track Land Reform Programme (FTLRP) as part of an attempt to speed

8. See Miller, "Doctrine of Discovery," 2; Charles, "Doctrine of Discovery."
9. Adebayo, *Curse of Berlin*.

up the return of land to the people.[10] However, on the international stage, Zimbabwe's FTLRP was mainly branded as a forceful, chaotic, and violent program that would only result in food insecurity, under-usage of land, a pariah state, economic collapse, and so on.[11] Furthermore, due to its FTLRP program Zimbabwe is suffering from harsh economic sanctions that threaten to collapse the Zimbabwean economy. However, the FTLRP was a step towards ensuring that land would not remain a commodity for a few white commercial farmers and agro-industrial estates by reversing the racial patterns on land ownership.[12]

Colonial Empire, Colonial Settler, and Indigenes: The Bible, Land, and Separation

For the colonial empires, the Bible was an instrument of social control in the subdued lands. In the context of settler colonialism, such as South Africa, the Bible was for the settlers an instrument of identity formation in the new land. It is no wonder that the land issue in the (South) African context is intricately linked with the issue of the racialization of society or body politics. The land issue had to do with who and where.

Afrikaners[13] (Colonial Settlers) and Identity Formation

Bosman notes that throughout their history Afrikaner resistance to the British empire can hardly be separated from the issue of biblical interpretation.[14] The Great Trek was one of the pillars in the development of the Afrikaner nationalist ideology. It was a heterogeneous movement that saw a substantial increase of white people in the interior of southern Africa as Afrikaners made their way from the colonially named Cape of Good Hope. It was a formative process that had as its scriptural foundation the exodus motif, as well as the Calvinist concepts of predestination and election. Afrikaners viewed their

10. See Matondi, *Zimbabwe's*, 19.

11. Matondi, *Zimbabwe's*, 6.

12. See Mkodzongi and Lawrence, "Fast Track," 1; Moyo, "Changing Agrarian Relations," 944.

13. The term *Afrikaner* became prominent by the end of the eighteenth century, when a new community emerged with its own identity and language as the Dutch or French or German peoples blended together (Giliomee, *Afrikaners*, 50–53).

14. Bosman, "Jerusalemgangers."

history as a sacred history, thereby regarding themselves as chosen people of God and regarding the African land in which they found themselves as their promised land.[15] Furthermore, the Afrikaners also established their foothold on the land through the naming of places. Names such as Jordan, Jericho, and Nylstroom evoke the exodus motif.

The Afrikaners were colonial settlers with their roots in Europe; in their attempt to establish themselves on the land, they found themselves in conflict not only with the indigenes, but also with the British colonial empire. Among Afrikaners existed marginal groups, such as the *Jerusalemgangers*, who created their own counter-narrative to the British empire as an imperial force, which they equated with the Pharaoh.[16] The conflict between the British and the Afrikaners was not limited to marginal groups. In the settler colony of South Africa, the Anglo-Boer War highlights a trajectory in which a white settler minority vied for political power against the British imperial power and the indigenous people.[17] This was not mere struggle for political power; it was at the same time a struggle for land as a place of habitat and a resource.

Afrikaner and Apartheid

The conviction that underlies the apartheid ideology is that ethnic diversity is in accordance with the will of God. It was, therefore, believed that for different ethnic groups to achieve God's purpose in a multinational country, they should pursue God along nationalistic and individualistic pathways. This ideology is intertwined with the land question, as it also had to do with who stays where in accordance with the land acts and acts regarding the separation of the ethnic groups. The white churches in South Africa, particularly the Afrikaans Reformed Churches (Dutch Reformed Church [DRC], also known as the Nederduitse Gereformeerde Kerk [NGK]; Gereformeerde Kerk in Suid Afrika [GKSA]; Nederduitse Hervormde Kerk [NHK]) supported the nationalistic ideals and provided the theological justification for them.[18]

15. Degenaar, "Philosophical Roots," 11–39.

16. Bosman, "Jerusalemangangers."

17. Mamdani, *Victims*, 104.

18. See Hermann, *The Afrikaners*, 482–86; Lategan, "Reading the Letter to the Galatians," 132. The biblical rationale for the Dutch Reformed Church's justification of apartheid is well documented. See Kinghorn, *Die NG Kerk en Apartheid*; De Gruchy, *Church*

The 1975 report of the Dutch Reformed Church, *Human Relations and the South African Scene*, was intended to provide the scriptural basis and expositional justification for apartheid. In the report, the church appealed to the following Scripture portions in support of the policy of independent, autogenous development of the different ethnic groups:[19]

Old Testament Texts

a. *Genesis 1:28; 9:1, 7*: the diversity of people is regarded as implicit in the fact of creation and the cultural injection, meaning God's command to multiply and fill the earth.[20]

b. *Genesis 11:1–9*: The deliberate concentration on one spot was regarded as in conflict with God's command to fill the earth. The differentiation of languages at the Tower of Babel is seen as a "spiritual" splitting of human into separate community units with the concomitant development of individual cultures and religions.[21]

c. *Deuteronomy 32:8 and Amos 9:7*: From these passages, it was argued that the Old Testament "fully accepts the reality of the existence of nations and peoples."[22] The report seems to recognize that Deut 32:8 does not provide firm support for the policy; however it proceeds to state, "[Deut 32:8] nevertheless seems to indicate that the fate of people is not beyond the will and intervention of God." Amos 9:7 is in support of this by stating that "on occasion, He even assigned each its own homeland."[23]

Based on these texts, the report concludes that "the differentiation of 'peoples' is implicit in the command of creation and that the events at Babel merely gave it a new momentum and character . . . Therefore we emphasize 'families', 'nations' and 'countries', with 'language' as an

---

Struggle; Dutch Reformed Church, Human, *Relations and South African*; Dutch Reformed Church, *Reply of the Dutch Reformed Church*; Landman, *A Plea for Understanding*.

19. The following works which provide a critique on use of the Bible in support of apartheid may be consulted: Vorster, "Bible and Apartheid," 94–111; Bax, "Bible and Apartheid," 112–143; Bax, *Different Gospel*.

20. Dutch Reformed Church, *Human Relations*, 14.

21. Dutch Reformed Church, *Human Relations*, 16.

22. Dutch Reformed Church, *Human Relations*, 23.

23. Dutch Reformed Church, *Human Relations*, 23.

important distinguishing factor."[24] Therefore, "[a] political system based on autogenous or separate development of various groups can be justified from the Bible."[25]

NEW TESTAMENT TEXTS

a. *Acts 2:5–13*: This passage (especially v. 6) was understood as confirming that indeed it is the will of God to have a diversity of people and that each man should learn the great deeds of God in his own language (see also Matt 28:19; Rom 1:16).[26]

b. *Acts 17:26*: This passage served to confirm the "fact that God appointed specific times for the various nations as well as the boundaries for their homelands."[27]

c. *Galatians 3:28, Colossians 3:11, 1 Corinthians 12:13*: The distinction between Israel and the nations, which existed in the Old Testament, is accepted as outdated. The New Testament ushers in "the new dispensation, national, cultural and biological factors" which overrides the differences.[28] There is now unity in Christ (Gal 3:28; Col 3:11) and in the Spirit (1 Cor 12:13). Such unity was viewed as unity in diversity, as it does not deny the existence of individuality and diversity.[29]

Based on these passages and others not referred to here, it is concluded that the New Testament assumes the existence of various nations "but never characterized it as sinful; nor does it call upon Christians to renounce their nationality."[30] This theology attempts to answer the question whether the diversity of peoples is in accordance to God's will and then proceed to show that the existence of different races and peoples is to be judged and evaluated positively. The adherents of this theology of apartheid boasted of the fact that they value the diversity of peoples positively and incorporate it in

---

24. Dutch Reformed Church, *Human Relations*, 20.

25. Dutch Reformed Church, *Human Relations*, 71.

26. Dutch Reformed Church, *Human Relations*, 43, 46, 87.

27. Dutch Reformed Church, *Human Relations*, 31.

28. Dutch Reformed Church, *Human Relations*, 29.

29. Dutch Reformed Church, *Human Relations*, 32.

30. Dutch Reformed Church, *Human Relations*, 31.

their ideas on relations between races and peoples, thereby distinguishing them from other Christians of other countries.[31]

The white church, with its justification of apartheid, was in a sense also justifying the dispossession of indigenous people of their land. As Mofokeng notes, "The white church became a wealthy and powerful beneficiary of blood land."[32]

Black Theology and the Bible:
The Struggle to Regain Stolen Land

Black theology in South Africa emerged in the late 1960s as an extension of the Black Consciousness Movement. Maimela identifies the following three trends:[33] the Black Solidarity trend (1970–1980), which emphasized white racism as the root cause of all evils in their social analysis of black oppression; the Black Solidarity-Materialist trend, which began to emerge in the late 1970s and argued that the former South African society should be viewed as basically a class society in which class divisions were determined by racial divisions; the Non-Racist trend, which began in the 1980s, the distinguishing feature being that it has softened the traditional black consciousness stand against alliances with the white "democrats" or "progressives." In the current post-colonial, post-apartheid period, there have been questions about the relevance of black theology, and a lot has been written in an attempt to justify its continuing relevance. Black theology is not a monolithic theology which simply says the same thing at all times,[34] and thus, while political freedom has been attained in the current context and there are mechanisms in place to redress the past injustice of stolen land, the land question has not been resolved. Therefore, in some sense, black theology's task is not complete, and I agree with Mosala's statement that "without liberating the land our people will never be genuinely liberated."[35] Below, we highlight the views on the Bible and land within black theology, black consciousness, and liberation as the centre of theology.

31. Dutch Reformed Church, *Human Relations*, 71.
32. Mofokeng, "Land Is Our Mother," 45.
33. Maimela, "Black Theology," 114–116. See also Maluleke, "Black theology,"
34. Maimela, "Black Theology," 114.
35. Mosala, "Land," 45.

The Land or the Bible or Both

The anecdote referred to earlier in this study regarding black people given the Bible and their land taken also speaks to the way the Bible is viewed among those whose land was taken. Thus, there is a sense in which even though the Bible is viewed as a problem, black people at the same time kept it in their hands. The anecdote, as Mofokeng argues, highlights the following, among other things: first, the central position occupied by the Bible in the colonization, oppression, and exploitation of the African people; second, the paradox of Africans converting to a religion of the oppressor and accepting the Bible, an instrument used in the colonization, oppression, and exploitation process.[36] For the colonizer and the colonized to share the same Bible and faith reflects, as West observes, both a historical crisis and a methodological crisis. The crisis is historical in that the Bible was used both as an instrument of social control and as an instrument of social struggle, and it is methodological in that the Bible is open to different interpretations; the biblical text is therefore both a problem and a solution.[37]

While the anecdote reflects a sad historical crisis, figures like Desmond Tutu tended to view having the Bible in black hands as positive, a "better deal." Having the Bible in the hands of the oppressed and marginalized implied that the oppressed had both the presence of God on their side and a primary resource for the struggle of liberation and survival.[38] Therefore, those who used the Bible to oppress others were viewed with suspicion, as their use of the Bible was regarded as misuse or misinterpretation of the Bible.[39] The Bible itself was not regarded as a problem, but it was the use of the Bible that was viewed as problematic.

In the early stages, black theologians tended to embrace the Bible as the Word of God and yet at the same time take the situation or context of readers as the starting point. Black theologians tended to view their task as being to reveal God's Word to the oppressed.[40] Dwane, for example, continues to argue that liberation theology, like any other theology, cannot

---

36. Mofokeng, "Black Christians," 34
37. West, *Biblical Hermeneutics*, 52.
38. Tutu, *Hope and Suffering*, 124–29; West, *The Academy of the Poor*, xi.
39. West, "Negotiating," 27.
40. Dwane, "Christology and Liberation," 30; Boesak, *Farewell to Innocence*, 16.

equate itself with the Gospel. Rather it is "concerned with the interpretation of the one Gospel for all sorts of conditions."[41]

In the late 1970s and 1980s, black theologians adopted Marxist presuppositions and analysis, and in turn, viewed the Bible as a problematic tool.[42] Mosala criticized Allan Boesak and Archbishop Desmond Tutu for drawing their hermeneutical assumption from white theology.[43] He argued that for black theology to be effective, it must break its ideological and theoretical links with white theology and Western civilization. By this, he implied a break from a view which takes the Bible as the starting point and a view of history that considers the Bible nonideological. For Mosala, a view that equates the Bible with the Word of God tends to endorse the view of the Bible held by the power elites. For Mosala, the Bible "offers no certain starting point . . . there is simply too much de-ideologization to be made before it can be hermeneutically straightforward in terms of the struggle for liberation."[44] Maluleke, following on Mosala's view, argues that the equation of the Bible with the Word of God is naïve and dangerous, as it often results in the equation of human views of the Bible with the Word of God.[45] The way forward, Maluleke, suggests, is to acknowledge that both our society and the Bible are sites of struggle.[46] Therefore, for Mosala and Maluleke, black theology has its roots in the Bible insofar as it is capable of linking our modern-day struggles against various forms of oppression with the struggles of the communities of the Bible.

Thus, black theology utilizes the Bible to get the land back through a materialistic reading of the Bible and a black conscious ideology.[47] For black theologians, it is not a matter of either the land or the Bible, but it is a matter of using the Bible as a weapon in the struggle to get the land back. Therefore, for the African Christian, the Bible is no mere book of faith which Africans have to read simply for spiritual upliftment; it is also a book that reminds the African that the land is lost.

41. Dwane, "Christology and Liberation," 30

42. See, Maimela, "Black Theology," 114; Parratt, "Marxist Trend," 78.

43. Mosala, *Biblical Hermeneutics.*

44. Mosala, *Biblical Hermeneutics,* 120–21.

45. Maluleke, "Black and African," 13.

46. Maluleke, "Black and African," 12.

47. Maluleke, "Postcolonial Mission,"

Black Consciousness: Consciousness of Being Landless

Black consciousness has to do with the black person's experience as he reacts to the life situation of domination, oppression, and discrimination by whites.[48] The term "black" is used as "encompassing all the different ethnic groups in the black community, sharing the solidarity of the oppressed."[49] Thus, the term is used as a symbol of oppression, also including Indians and Coloureds as part of the oppressed. Black theology, therefore, seeks to interpret God's activity or God's Word from black experiences.[50] However, for others, it is the black experience which should be taken as the starting point in interpreting the Bible. For still others, the underlying presupposition is that divine revelation happens within a specific social context.[51] Therefore, the black experience of landlessness serves as a perspective through which the Bible is read. In a sense, the Bible becomes an instrument in black hands to regain stolen land.

Liberation as the Center of Christian Theology

Within black theology, "liberation" is taken as the central message of the gospel or a theological centre of Christian theology.[52] With liberation as the central motif, the following themes emanate:

- God is the Liberator, revealed in a situation of oppression (Exod 2:24–25; 15:1–2; 19:4–5; 20:3, etc.). The "exodus" motif, as Boesak argues, runs through the Scripture; it is reiterated in the Psalms and

---

48. Kretzschmar points out that "the Black Consciousness Movement was not a purely secular movement, from the outset, it encompassed very definite religious elements and implications." Black Theology came to represent the theological dimension of Black Consciousness (Kretzschmar, *The Voice of Black Theology*, 60–61).

49. Boesak, *Farewell to Innocence*, 109. Gqubule, "What is Black Theology?" 19.

50. Baartman, "Significance," 20.

51. Kiogora, "Black Hermeneutics," 345. Boesak states, "The black situation is that situation within which reflection and action take place, but it is the Word of God, which illuminates the reflection and guides the action. . . God, it seems to us, reveals Himself in the situation, the Word is being heard in the situation, thereby giving meaning to the situation. The black experience provides the framework within which blacks understand the revelation in Jesus Christ. No more, no less" (Boesak, *Farewell to Innocence*, 16).

52. Cone, *A Black Theology*, 5; Boesak, *Farewell to Innocence*, 19.

actualized in the prophets, and thus the "liberation message was the centre and sustenance of the life of Israel."[53]

- God is on the side of the poor (Isa 3:13–15; Prov 17:5; 19:17; 23:10–11; etc.). Cone argues that God is on the side of the poor and defenceless.[54] Tutu states, "Oppressed peoples must hear that, according to the Bible, this God is always on the side of the downtrodden. He is graciously on their side not because they are more virtuous and better than their oppressors, but solely and simply because they are oppressed, he is that kind of a God . . . Those whom God has saved must become the servants of others, for they are saved ultimately not for their self-aggrandizement or self-glorification, but so that they may bring others to a saving knowledge."[55]

- The God revealed in Jesus Christ is a liberating God (Isa 61:1–12; Luke 4:18–19; 11:20; Matt 15:30; etc.). Boesak states, "Just as in the Old Testament, the message of liberation forms the *cantus firmus* of the proclamation of the New Testament. Jesus did not alienate Himself from the prophetic proclamation of liberation.[56]

The structuring of the biblical content around a theological centre is not a foreign practice in biblical theology. Black theology is a theology of liberation. It calls for an understanding of the historical situation in which it is addressed. Thus, it can be understood as a situational theology or contextual theology.[57]

However, as Mosala argues, black theology, particularly in its materialistic approach, is not so much interested in prescribing which texts should be read. The hermeneutical problem is not solved by choosing some "right" text for one's struggle or situation; rather, the hermeneutic approaches the Bible informed by the struggles and experiences of ordinary people and confronts the text to expose the politics and ideologies underlying the text; it reads the text against the grain, going behind the text and through the

53. Boesak, *Farewell to Innocence*, 20–21.

54. Cone, *God of the Oppressed*.

55. Tutu, "Theology of Liberation," 166.

56. Cone states, "If the history of Israel and the New Testament description of the historical Jesus reveal that God is a God who is identified with Israel because it is an oppressed community, the resurrection of Jesus means that all the oppressed peoples become his people. Herein lies the universal note implied in the gospel message of Jesus (Cone, *A Black Theology of Liberation*, 3).

57. Boesak, *Farewell to innocence*, 17–19.

gaps, avoiding colluding with the voices of the elite, the ruling, dominant, and oppressive class.[58] As Mosala cautions, the interpreters do not have to embrace the dominant/oppressive ideologies in the text. The fact that the interpreter may read texts that promote oppressive ideologies in liberative ways should not deceive the interpreter into thinking that oppressive texts can be totally tamed or subverted into liberative texts.[59]

Freedom in the Land: Theology of Reconstruction

The attainment of political freedom by African states ushered in a new era in African soil. In the context of South Africa, the last African state to gain freedom, the fall of the colonial-apartheid regime was an epoch event comparable with other global epochal events. This moment, as Villa-Vicencio views it, was a Kairos moment which required "a new social vision" and a "discovering of a new soul."[60] In the area of theology or biblical scholarship, others proposed a theological shift from the paradigm of black theology of liberation to a new paradigm of theology of reconstruction.

The Kenyan scholar Jesse N. K. Mugambi is recognized as the pioneer of the theology of reconstruction, which he proposed at the All Africa Conference of Churches (AACC) in 1990. However, it was after the AACC conference that Mugambi's theology of reconstruction started gaining traction. Mugambi argues, "Reconstruction is the new priority for African nations in the 1990s. The churches and their theologians will need to respond to this new priority in relevant fashion, to facilitate this process of reconstruction. The process will require considerable efforts of reconciliation and confidence-building. It will also require orientation and retraining."[61] For Mugambi, the underlying presupposition is that the political transition from colonial oppression ushered in a new era which required a move beyond the liberation paradigm. The shift from the liberation paradigm to a reconstruction paradigm entailed a shift from the Moses-Aaron paradigm to an Ezra–Nehemiah paradigm.[62] In the South African context, Villa-Vicencio championed the course for the theology of reconstruction.

58. Mosala, "Land," 44; Maluleke, "Postcolonial Mission," 523.

59. Mosala, *Biblical Hermeneutics*, 30.

60. Villa-Vicencio, "Keeping the Revolution," 51. See also Petersen, "Non-racialism," 18.

61. Mugambi, "Future," 36.

62. See Mugambi, *Christian Theology*; Mugambi, "Religion," Mugambi, *From*

Below are some of the key tenets of the theology of reconstruction in contrast to black theology of liberation.

Black Theology of Liberation	Reconstruction Theology
Focus is on Moses and the exodus motif	Focus is on Ezra–Nehemiah (and other post-exilic texts such as Jeremiah, Ezekiel, Deutero-Isaiah) and nation building
Moses–Aaron leadership: Leaders who do not enter the Promised Land	Ezra–Nehemiah: Leaders who returned to the land (post-exilic period)
• Moses was trained in Pharaoh's court.	• Nehemiah rose through the ranks in the Babylonian court.
• Moses led through managerial training and skill.	• Nehemiah did not have to do the work himself; he mobilized everyone.
• There is anarchy in the absence of the leader.	• Nehemiah inspired the people through encouragement, not commands, as in the case of Moses.
Focus is on resistance	Focus is on nation-building
No-saying to all forms of exploitation: Theology of negation	Yes-saying to meaningful efforts in nation-building: positive and constructive theology
Opposed to the colonial-oppressive state	In critical solidarity with the state in the new social order
Past-sensitive	Future sensitive
Focus is on the oppressor	Focus on the liberated agent

The focus of reconstruction theology is the understanding of the concept of land in light of the post-exilic situation, with a special focus on the return-ees from exile.[63] The return from exile is, thus, viewed as ushering in a new era in which the returnees engage in nation-building. However, the focus is not merely on Old Testament texts; the New Testament also receives attention, with a focus on the ministry of Jesus and his teachings, with particular reference to the Sermon on the Mount, Matthew 5–7, which is considered

---

Liberation, Mugambi, "Future."

63. See Villa-Vicencio, *Theology of Reconstruction*, 26.

a reconstructive theological text.[64] For Mugambi, Jesus was more a "reconstructionist" than a "liberationist."[65] The theology of reconstruction calls upon the previously oppressed to be initiatave and take responsibility in rebuilding their land. While reconstruction theology has gained some level of support over the years, it has also been met with criticism. Dube particularly points out that the separation between liberation and reconstruction creates the impression that liberation is something to be transcended.[66] She further highlights that reconstructionist theologians tend to overlook issues of justice, considering the fact that the Ezra–Nehemiah text is a colonizing and gender-oppressive text.[67] In a similar vein, Farisani highlights that the reconstructionist theologians tend to ignore the ideological biases of the text towards the returnees from exile at the expense of the ʿam ha-aretz (people of the land). The ideology behind the conflict between the returning exiles and the ʿam ha-aretz is an oppressive one.[68]

It should be added that reconstruction theology tends to presume that the colonial enterprise came to an end once the colonial empires withdrew from the colonies. While the political withdrawal of colonial empires from Africa was monumental, it did not amount to the evaporation of the structures of colonialism—the historical legacy of colonialism still influences African countries. As decolonial scholars warn us, the colonial matrix of power is still with us. Therefore, it is misguided to think that either the liberation project or the decolonial project is complete.

Freedom in our context remains incomplete for as long as the land issue is not resolved. In the Zimbabwean context, the slow progress of the land reform eventually led to the Fast Track Land Reform Programme, which amounted to seizures of farmlands from the whites—a process which to some extent was violent towards those white farmers who resist the takeover of their farms. In the South African context, the so-called

64. Mugambi, "Theology of Reconstruction," 147–48; Mwuara, "Reconstruction Mission," 4.

65. Mugambi, "Theology of Reconstruction," 147–48.

66. Dube, "Jesse Mugambi," 4. Similarly, Vellem argues that for reconstructionist theologians to argue for a shift from liberation to reconstruction is substantially different from arguing that liberation should be the starting point for reconstruction: "Liberation is the comprehensive framework within which reconstruction and development can find their place" (Vellem, "Ideology," 549).

67. Dube, "Jesse Mugambi."

68. Farisani, "Ideologically Biased"; Farisani, "Use of Ezra–Nehemiah"; Farisani, "Black Biblical Hermeneutics."

"willing-buyer willing-seller" has failed to yield results, eventually leading to the push towards a constitutional amendment that would allow for
the government to re-take land without compensation. The decolonial
process in the South African context remains "incomplete," and therefore,
it is proper to speak in Fanonian terms of "incomplete liberation."[69] The
incompleteness of liberation is evident at multiple levels—the failure to
return stolen land, the high rate of inequality, the reproduction of colonial-
apartheid social and spatial exclusion, xenophobic violence, and so on. All
these threaten to reverse the gains of the liberation struggle.

Decolonial Reflection on the Theme
of Promised Land in the Hexateuch

This section of the study is a reflection on the motif of land promise in the
Hexateuch from a decolonial perspective. The theme of land within the
Hexateuch and broadly within the Old Testament is multifaceted, and it
would therefore not be possible to deal with all the aspects related to the
theme of land.[70] This study argues that the land of promise motif cannot
be divorced from issues of imperial forces, which shaped Israel/Judah's relations with other nations. The Hexateuch reflects two main perspectives
of the acquisition of the land of promise: first, an anticolonial or counter-
imperial view of land acquisition through negotiations for space in a space
already occupied by others, and second, a colonial perspective of land
acquisition from the position of power through military conquest. Thus,
the Hexateuch, in its final form, is plurivoiced. It contains not only voices
supporting the imperial ideology of conquest, dispossession, enslavement,
and elimination, but also alternative voices of negotiation, accommoda-
tion, and freedom of movement.

One of the prevailing positions in recent studies of the Pentateuch is
that the Pentateuch is a product of the Persian period,[71] which others take
further to imply also that the Pentateuch was produced under Persian imperial authorization.[72] For those who regard the Pentateuch as produced

69. Fanon, *Black Skins*, 4.

70. See, among others, Brueggeman, *The Land*; Habel, *The Land is Mine*; Wright,
God's People.

71. See, among others, Blenkinsopp, "Was the Pentateuch Civic"; Otto, "Forschungen"; Ska, *Introduction*; Schmid, "The Late Persian Formation"; Kratz, "Pentateuch."

72. See among others Frei, *Die Persische Reichsautorisation*; Frei, "Persian Imperial

under Persian imperial authorization, the Pentateuch is an example of a legal document through which the Persian empire exercised some form of control over those in Yehud. However, others rather opt to view the Pentateuch as produced under the influence of the Persian empire, but not as an imperial legal document to regulate life over those in Yehud. Ska writes,

> The primary purpose of the Pentateuch, for whoever reads it as a whole, is not to regulate life within the province of the Persian empire but to define the conditions of membership in a specific community called "Israel." There are two primary conditions: blood ties and a "social contract." Genealogies establish the blood ties. The members of Israel are descendants of Abraham, Isaac, and Jacob. The "social contract" is the Covenant, with all the rights and duties, both religious and civil, that it entails.[73]

In this study, we follow the view that the Pentateuch should be viewed as a compromise document in which competing ideological views are brought together,[74] and furthermore, we make a literary compromise in terms of separating the Pentateuch as Torah from the books from Joshua to Kings.[75]

Pitkänen argues that the Pentateuch–Joshua should be viewed as a "settler-colonial document" which is "at least partially an ideological blueprint for settler colonialism associated with the ancient highlands of Canaan at the end of the second millennium BCE."[76] While Pitkänen's view has merit, the Pentateuch–Joshua or Hexateuch does not appear to be shaped by just one ideology. The Hexateuch is not single-voiced; rather, it is a plurivoiced text. As I will point out, the book of Genesis, particularly the patriarchal narrative, at some level is not shaped by the colonial ideology of supplanting the other; rather, it reflects an anti-colonial ideology of land as space and resource available for sharing with others—which can be negotiated.

Authorisation"; Knoppers, *An Achaemenid Imperial Authorization*; Hagerdorn, "Persia and Torah"; Blum, *Studien zur Komposition*, 333–60, Crusemann, "Le Pentateugue," 339–60.

73. Ska, *Introduction*, 225–26.

74. See, for example, Schmid, *Genesis and the Moses Story*.

75. See, for example, Römer, "How Many Books (Teuchs)."

76. Pitkänen, "Pentateuch–Joshua," 252.

Genesis 12–50 (Patriarchal Narrative): Promised Land as Negotiated Land

Schmid argues that the Genesis narrative—in particular, the patriarchal narrative (Genesis 12–50)—did not always serve as the introduction of the Exodus story and following.[77] The origin of Israel was in the strict sense from Egypt. The two strands, patriarchal narrative and the exodus story, present two different perspectives on Israel's origins. However, in this study, we are more interested on the land motif as projected in the two strands.

In the patriarchal narrative, the promise of land is first given to Abraham (Gen 12:1–3, 7; 15:7, 18; 17:18), then to Isaac (Gen 26:3), and then to Jacob (Gen 28:13; 35:12). Within the patriarchal narrative, Abraham is called by the deity from an unknown land to an unknown land:

> Now YHWH said to Abram, "Leave your country, your fellow people, your father's house to the land that I will show you."

The promise inaugurates a migration of Abram from his land to another land. The land of promise in the so-called Priestly material is identified as the "land of Canaan."[78]

The migrant Abram is presented as having freedom of movement in and out of the land, as do Isaac[79] and Jacob. The ancestors live in peaceful coexistence with those who were already in the land. The migrants do not pose a threat to the inhabitants of the land. As Wöhrle argues,

> According to P, the existence of the people who already lived in the land before the ancestors came to it is not presented as being a temporary fact which has to be overcome. The land is given to the ancestors not instead of the people of the land, but in addition to these people.[80]

Those already in the land are projected as willing to share the land with those who come into the land, both in the land of promise and in Egypt, and in both Priestly and non-Priestly strand. In the land of promise at Gerar, Abimelech is willing to share the land with Abraham: "And Abimelech said, 'My land is before you; live wherever you like'" (Gen 20:13).

77. Schmid, *Genesis and the Moses Story.*

78. Gen 12:4b–5; 13:6, 11–12.

79. Isaac has freedom to move, though when he wants to leave for Egypt, he is instructed by the deity not to (Gen 26:2).

80. Wöhrle, "The Un-Empty Land," 204.

At Shechem, Jacob and his family settle next to the city of Shechem; however, inasmuch as something goes wrong in the relationship as Dinah is raped, there is an invitation to intermarry and live together: "But Hamor said to them, 'Intermarry with us; give us your daughters and take our daughters for yourselves. You can settle among us; the land is open to you. Live in it, trade in it, and acquire property in it'" (Gen 34:9–10, NIV). In Egypt, Pharaoh is willing to share the land with Joseph and his family: "Pharaoh said to Joseph, 'Your father and your brothers have come to you, and the land of Egypt is before you; settle your father and your brothers in the best part of the land'" (Gen 47:5–6). In all the settlement notices of the patriarchs, there is no conquest of the people as a means of supplanting the original inhabitants of the land.

There is strife over resources among the migrants themselves, Abram and Lot (Gen 13); however, the strife does not lead to a supplanting of the inhabitants of the land in order to gain the resources of the land. The strife over resources between the migrants and inhabitants of the land do not result in the inhabitants being supplanted from their land (Gen 21:16–34 and 26:1–31); instead, they are resolved peacefully through negotiation and treaties (Gen 21:31–32; 26:30–31). The patriarchs are accommodated in the land of others with whom they negotiate for settlement and purchase of land. The patriarchs are thus not the powerful invaders who come to take over the land.

The patriarchal narrative resonates with the exilic and postexilic period, at a time when the Davidic monarchy was no more, with the exiles given room to return to their land, and yet with the freedom to continue to live as diaspora under the Persian empire.[81] The family ties as projected in the patriarchal narratives are not limited to those in the land of promise, but extend to those outside of the land of promise in Paddan Aram (Gen 25:20; 28:21–27). Isaac and Jacob both marry from their relatives who live outside of the promised land. Jacob's children, except for Benjamin, are born outside of the land in Paddan Aram, and furthermore, he accumulates his wealth in Paddan Aram (outside of the promised land). Yet he is insistent on returning to the land to return to the land of promise. The family ties outside of the land are not limited to Paddan Aram, that is, in the Mesopotamian area. The Joseph story, which is embedded within the Jacob cycle extends the family ties to Egypt. Also notable, the patriarchs

---

81. See also Albertz, *Israel in Exile*, 246, Kiefer, *Exil und Diaspora*, 107.

are assured of YHWH's presence in the land and outside of the land (Gen 46; 39:1–6, 45:8).[82]

The relationship between Esau/Edom and Jacob/Judah is presented as one of strife. Yet the patriarchal narrative also projects it as a story of reconciliation and peaceful co-existence between the twins. Thus, for the patriarchal narrative, the story of the twins is more than just an aetiology on the conflict between the two; furthermore, it may also be viewed as an attempt to heal the conflict. If Edom wronged Judah during the time of exile, Judah has to recall as well the wrong inflicted on Edom. The age-old conflict between the twins can be overcome; however, the responsibility also lies on the one who was wronged to forgive and enter into a fresh relationship with the other.

The patriarchal narrative should be viewed as an attempt at establishing a new system of relating with the other in the face of a Persian colonial empire, which established its rule through and authority over its subjects not through the determination or imposition of where the colonial subjects should settle, but maintained its rule the indigenous rulers and the colonial middlemen. While the Persian empire ushered in a new era, the empire's policies produced structural inequalitis and allowed for the realization of the "holy seed" ideology and the attendant. However, within the Yehud community as described in Ezra–Nehemiah, the dominant ideology, as Brett points out, was that of exclusion of those who were not considered to be "holy seed."[83] The theological construction of "holy seed" was part of a ploy to gain an advantage in a context of limited land and resources. This, in Johnson's terms, was the "pattern of Othering in antiquity," as the group that had lost economic and political power engage in stereotyping the Other.[84] However, within the imperial matrix of power, even the so-called "holy seed" was still in the realm of the exploited, as they had to service the empire with the proceeds from the land.

Exodus to Joshua (Exodus and Conquest): Promised Land as Conquered Land

The literary complex from Exodus to Joshua, as already noted, may be viewed as projecting its own understanding of the origins of Israel. The

82. Albertz, *Israel in Exile*, 267–68.
83. Brett, "Reading the Bible," 51.
84. Johnson, *Holy Seed*, 78.

Exodus to Joshua story is shaped on the motif of exodus–*eisodos*, which turns the Canaanites into victims of the conquest—they are evildoers whose land can be taken with impunity (Deut 9:4–6; 20:17–18). The exodus from Egypt to the promised land (the land of others) makes YHWH both the deliverer and the conqueror.[85] The story of the God who is on the side of the oppressed turns on its head to become the story of the God who is on the side of the oppressor.

The Exodus to Joshua story, as Pitkänen argues, is based on the ideology of settler colonialism, which should not be viewed as simply characteristic of modern European colonization; it was also present in ancient times.[86] Settler colonialism, as Wolfe highlights, "is a structure, not an event."[87] In settler colonialism, the colonialists come to stay and to establish their own social, political, and religious order in the colonised land. Thus, the colonial settlers are unlike the colonial sojourners and middlemen (colonial administrators, military personnel, entrepreneurs, adventurers, religious people, and so on), who are there to serve the interests of the colonial empire.[88]

In the South African context, both settler colonialism and colonial empire were operative—the colonial settlers had their own interests in the land and, therefore, clashed with the interest of the British empire, which wanted to serve its interests through its sojourners and middlemen. However, following the Anglo-Boer War, the two colluded to form the Union of South Africa, which was intended to serve the interest of both colonial settler and colonial empire. The indigenous people were left holding the short end of the sick as the colonialists fought for ownership and control of the land.

Pitkänen, following Day's characteristics of settler colonialism, characterizes Israel as a colonialist settler community that utilized overlapping strategies in the process of supplanting other nations that were already established in the land of promise:[89]

   a. *Establishing a legal claim over the land.* The link between Genesis traditions, such as the building of altars (Gen 12:6–7; 13:18; 21:33; 35:1–7) and the buying of a tract of land for the burial of Sarah (Gen

85. Warrior, "Canaanites, Cowboys, and Indians," 8.
86. Pitkänen, "Pentateuch–Joshua," 251.
87. Wolfe, 'Settler colonialism" 388; and Wolfe, 'Structure and event," 123.
88. Veracini, *Settler Colonialism*, 6.
89. See Pitkänen, "Pentateuch–Joshua," 253–62.

23), serve the "genocidal imperative." The building of monuments, e.g., Gilgal (Josh 3–4), the heap of stones over Achan (Josh 7:26), and the monument at Geliloth (Josh 22), serve to legitimate the possession of the land through collective memory.

b. *Mapping the land* as a process of "knowing the land" and of imposing borders (Gen 12:6–9; 13:17; Num 13–14; Josh 2; 18:3–10; 20–21).

c. *Claiming by naming.* Naming and/or renaming is part of laying claim to the settled land, e.g., Gilgal (Josh 14:15), Hill of Foreskins (Josh 5:2–3), Valley of Achor (Josh 7:26), Hebron (Josh 14:15; 15:13; Judg 1:10), Debir (Josh 15:15), Jerusalem (Judg 19:10), Bethel (Judg 1:23), Dan (Josh 19:47; Judg 18:19), Havvoth Jair (Num 32:31), and Nobah (Num 3:42).

d. *Foundation stories.* These stories are intended to establish legitimacy over the land in the minds of the colonialists and the minds of others by linking the people to the land in meaningful ways.[90] Examples are the land promised to the fathers (Exod 3:16–17, 4:5; Deut 1:8; 6:10; 9:5; 29:13; 30:20), the exodus story, law-giving at Sinai, wanderings in the wilderness. Furthermore, the genealogies serve to establish Israel's place among the nations and the land that Israel occupies.

e. *Supplanting the savages and the genocidal imperative.* The idea here is that certain people's lives are of a lower worth and they are therefore killable. Canaan is portrayed as cursed (Gen 9:25), and therefore certain nations are portrayed as killable, thus justifying the genocide in the book of Joshua.

f. *Justly conquering.* The land of Canaan is portrayed as to belonging to the Israelites through the right of conquest; however, in this case, the conquest is legitimised by YHWH.

g. *Tilling the soil and peopling the land.* The supplanting society lays claims to the land through developing the place (Josh 17:14–18) and bringing people into the land to take over the land and infrastructure already there (Num 21:25; Deut 6:10; Josh 24:13).

h. *Defending the territory.* The supplanting society takes over and is willing to defend its conquered territories (Num 32).

90. Day, *Conquest*, 136.

i. *Organizing the supplanting society.* The supplanting society not only seeks to eliminate the other society but also to replace its institutions.[91] The conquering Israelites were supposed to destroy established forms of worship in the land and establish their worship of YHWH (Deut 7:5).

In the context of the Exodus–Joshua narrative, the success of settler colonialism is in its gradual conquest of the "land of Canaan" turning it into "Israel" (etiologically the name given to the patriarch, Jacob) or "land of Israel" (a concept that only appears once within the framework of the Ennaeteuch, in 1 Sam 13:19).

The conquest model in the Exodus–Joshua narrative, while it is the dominant ideology within the Hexateuch, it is not the sole ideology; thus, a decolonial alternative is also evident in the text although suppressed. The negotiation model as projected in the patriarchal narrative presents an alternative view to the conquest model. In the South African context of settler colonialism, the negotiation model provibes a viable decolonial option in addressing the land issue. However, unlike in the patriarchal narratives in which the migrants negotiate to be accommodated in the territorories of the others, in our context it is the native people who have to negotiate to get their land back from the settler colonialists and do so under the prescripts of the laws which are part and parcel of the legacy of colonialism. The conquest model as projected in the Exodus–Joshua is an oppressive model which leaves us in sympathy with the Canaanites who were dispossessed of their land. Therefore, the question becomes: Can the Canaanites get their land back from the colonial settlers?

If the Exodus–Joshua text was the end of the story, one would conclude that the colonial settler movement into the promised land was a complete success (Josh 21:43–45). However, the biblical narrative is not single-voiced on the matter. The settler colonialists were met with resistance in the land of Canaan, whether overtly or subtly. As Veracini notes,

> Differently organised groups develop distinct anticolonial responses . . . Resistance and survival are thus the weapons of the colonised and the settler colonised; it is resistance and survival that make certain that colonialism and settler colonialism are never ultimately triumphant.[92]

91. Wolfe, "Structure and Event," 103.
92. Veracini, "Introduction," 3–4.

The subtle subversion that is highlighted in the book of Joshua is that of the Gibeonites, who deceived the colonial settlers (Josh 9). Therefore, the colonial settler could not take over the land of the Gibeonites. However, the Gibeonites were not the only survivors, and so Joshua warns the Israelites to remember the allotment of the land of the nations that still remained (23:4–5). The failure of the settler colonialism in the land of Canaan is also a recurring feature in the book of Judges. From a literary perspective, Pentateuch as "torah" serves as the measuring stick to judge the success and failure of Israel's nation during the conquest and in the settlement in the land.

The Exodus–Joshua narrative projects a land conquest ideology which was shaped by colonial or imperial thinking. This is not to say that the land of Canaan was taken over through the magnitude of force and violence as described in the Joshua narrative; rather, the Exodus–Joshua story serves as a story through which Israel attempted to assert its position in the world using an imperial ideology. The language used in the Exodus–Joshua narrative to project Israel as having an army of over six hundred thousand moving for a clean sweep in the land of Canaan is at best hyperbolic and reflects one of the ancient Near Eastern conceptualization of land attainment beyond the conquer and rule ideology.

Decolonization in the context of settler colonialism, according to Veracini, is "at best irrelevant and at worst detrimental to the indigenous peoples in settler societies."[93] For Veracini, the way that settler colonialism operates is that it aims at extinguishing the colonial-settler dynamic; the struggle against settler colonialism should be to keep the settler-indigenous relationship ongoing. This is because "settler colonialism ends with an indigenous ultimate permanence."[94] Thus, settler colonialism's success lies in its naturalization of the settler. While, it may be agreed with Veracini that settler colonialism operates differently from classic colonialism, it does not, however, render decolonization irrelevant in the context of settler colonialism. The decolonial project is not simply interested in attaining political freedom, that of not being ruled from the outside; in the South African context, it also implies dismantling the apartheid government and established rule from the inside. The decolonial project is interested in uncovering and exposing the continuing structures of settler colonialism that continue to shape the African context. The issue of land is but one example of the continuing pattern of settler colonialism; if this is disturbed, the international community,

93. Veracini, "Introduction," 6.
94. Veracini, "Introduction," 7.

the former colonisers, are swift to impose harsh sanctions, as is the case with Zimbabwe. Therefore, the demise of classical colonialism through the withdrawal of direct rule does not imply that the former colonial powers no longer rule—they rule indirectly through the structures of coloniality which classical colonialism and settler colonialism established.

In the South African context, the attempt to redress the land issue is through the land reform programme with its three pronged strategy—land restitution, land tenure reform and land resdistribution. However, the slow pace of land redistribution has resulted in disappointment and dissatisfaction as some communities still wait for the return of their lands. The land remains a promised deferred there are many whose lands are yet to be returned. A *Tshivenḓa* proverb comes to mind here, *thovhele ndi mma, ndi a ḓa ndi a ḓa, nwana avhuya a bebwa a tshimbila,* which may be rendered, "the king is a mother who says 'I am coming, I coming' and the child is born and starts walking." The meaning of the proverb is basically that leaders tend to promise things that they do not fulfil.

A decolonial theology of land in our African context should pursue decolonial justice, which is informed by the following, among other things: First, it seeks to disrupt and unmask the perpetuation of colonial structures which continually push those whose land was stolen to the zone of non-being. The long wait of the many for their land to be returned indicates the willingness of our African people to negotiate with those the dispossessed them of their land. However, from our African context, the concern is not the biblical land or Palestine rather the biblical theology of land simply provides one lens from a perspective of faith through which we attempt to grapple with our own realities relating to our land—the immediate reality, and from that also think of the land in the broader sense of our being in creation in our interconnectedness and shared responsibility towards the land. Therefore, a theology of land in our context should not ignore the European colonial dispossession our the indiginoues people of their land and the continuing structures of colonialism that continue to render the indigenous people landless in the so-called post-colonial period.

For those in Palestine, the biblical promised land is the reality in which they live. Therefore, as Raheb argues the land cannot be disconnected from its native people. However, as Raheb warns, it is an error to simply equate the Israeli people of today with the biblical Israelites as though they are the only ones with the rightful claim to the land and no other. The theology of the land in the context of Palestine cannot ignore the changing dynamics in history both in biblical times and after and the shifting identity of those who occupied the land. Therefore, a theology of land that ignores the Palestinians as the native people of the land, be they Muslims, Christians, Jews, and Samaritans). Thus, a theology of the biblical land, as Raheb argues, should also listen to the voices of the native people of the land, the Palestinians, heeding the cry from the oppression of the Jewish colonial settlers. Therefore, in our struggle for land in the South African context, we stand in solidarity with the Palestinian people who are dispossessed of their land—an act that is symbolized visually by a wall of injustice. Therefore, the wall of injustice must fall.

Second, decolonial theology of land requires a commitment to social justice past and present. The continuing landlessness of our people in (South) Africa is not accidental—it has historical roots. As García-Johnson notes, European colonialism transformed local European kings and kingdom into "global landlords" whereas the indigenous kings and their kingdom were forcefully and violently turned into the "global labor force and landless people." The dispossession of Africans from their land and elsewhere be it in the Americas and Australia through European colonialism was an act of injustice and dehumanization of the other. I concur with García-Johnson's view that a decolonial theology requires *myth-busting* as the colonialists created myth that served to facilitate the dispossession of land. In solidarity with the Palestanians, the colonial Jewish state also has to be denounce as it flies under the myth of the Jewish people as the sole rightful owners of the land at the neglect of other inhabitants of the land. In the South African context the failure of the democratic state to adequately address the challenge of landlessness of our people requires radical measures to be taken in order to address the challenge. If the constitution proves to be a hindrance in addressing the current landlessness, an amendment of such a constitution is a step in the right direction. Constitutional amendment is a negotiated process that allows for public engagement. However, the current debate on expropriation of land without compensation is in some sense misguided as the concept of "expropriation" tends to give the impression that the colonial settlers rightfully own the land—the possession of title deed in this case makes one a rightful owner whose rights to property have to protected by law (see Expropriation Act 63 of 1975 and RSA Constitution, 1996, Section 25). It is a *myth* that if the land is returned to its rightful owners it will threaten foreign investments and food security. It is the structures of coloniality flying under the banner of sanctions from those who had colonised our lands that threaten economies of countries that take radical steps to address the land issue.

Third, decolonial theology of land should be informed by indigenous knowledge by rooting itself in the African worldview. A decolonial theology of land has to take into consideration African conception of land and does not merely have to be informed by the biblical conception of land. In the South African contexs, our different cultures presents us with multiple views through which land theology can be developed. In my culture land is *ifa ḽashu* ("our inheritance") for us to live in, live from it, share it with other beings, and hand it to the next generation. When we die we join *vhaḽhasi* ("those below" or "ancestors"), whose presence is written all over our land. The Tshivenda saying *lupfumo lu mavuni* ("wealth is in the land") highlights the interconnectedness between people, land, and wealth. People do not exist in a vacuum, they exist in time and space, and so the land, as the space, is viewed as the primary mode of economic wellbeing and existence. While the land does supply its inhabitance with its delicacies and its resources, both men and women also have to work the land in order to produce wealth. Thus, from the perspective of the Vhavenḓa people land is the basic necessity for generating a thriving economy.

Fourth, decolonial theology of land must reject the normalization of the dispossession of land by rejecting the notion that the status quo is irreversible. The commitment to decolonial justice requires us to be aware that in settler colonialism, the structures of colonialism are so embedded in us that what we see is our naturalization into the settlers' system, while the settlers are not naturalised into our indigenous system. We have become subsumed under the settlers' system to an extent that our attempts to resolve the land issue are also intended to appease those who dispossessed us of our land. Decolonial justice would require a shift of land from the settlers back to the indigenous people. The power shift, however, does not imply the trading of one oppressor for another, with the previously oppressed becoming the new oppressors. It is the commitment to build a new world in which dispossession of land is not the norm—this considering the new land grabbers who are sweeping across Africa and elsewhere: the Gulf sheiks, Chinese state corporations, Wall Street speculators, Russian oligarchs, Indian microchip billionaires, doomsday fatalists, Midwestern missionaries, and City of London hedge-fund slickers.[95] Therefore, Africans cannot afford to pray with their eyes closed.

95. Pearce, *The Land Grabbers*, vii–x.

Conclusion

In developing a land theology, it is essential that we take into consideration the prism through which such theology is developed. A theology of land developed from an imperial position serves the interests of the empire, and it fosters dominance, oppression, exploitation, enslavement, displacement, expulsion, and genocide in order to serve the interests of the powerful. Such a theology of land perpetuates colonial ideology in which the conqueror takes all.

In our context, we require a decolonial theology of land that takes as its preferential option the damned—those whose land was stolen through the colonial machinery. Thus, in developing such a theology, it would be essential to consider the dynamics of power within the biblical texts and also those that shaped the producers of the biblical texts. In the South African context, a decolonial theology of the land cannot ignore the legacy of colonialism and apartheid that rendered the landless while granting the colonial settlers the privilege of landownership and permanence. Futhermore, our African conception of land has to inform our reading of the biblical text and our relationship with the land.

For Further Reading

Evers, Sandra, Caroline Seagle, Frouke Krijenburg, eds. *Africa for Sale? Positioning the State, Land and Society in Foreign Large-Scale Land Acquisition in Africa*. Afrika-Stuiecentrum Series 29. Leiden: Brill, 2013.

Havea, Jione, ed. *People and Land: Decolonizing Theologies*. Theology in the Age of Empire. Lanham, MD: Fortress Academic, 2020.

Masenya, Madipoane (Ngwan'a Mphahlele) and Hulisani Ramantswa. "Lupfumo lu Mavuni (Wealth Is in the Land): In Search for the Promised Land (Exo 3–4) in the Post-Colonial, Post Apartheid South Africa." *Journal of Theology for Southern Africa* 151 (2015) 96–116.

Mtshiselwa, Ndikho. *To Whom Belongs the Land? Leviticus 25 in an Africanist Liberationist Reading*. Bible and Theology in Africa 23. New York: Lang, 2017.

Ntreh, Benjamin A., Mark S. Aidoo, and Daniel N. A. Aryeh, eds. *Essays on the Land, Ecotheology, and Traditions in Africa*. Eugene, OR: Resource Publications, 2019.

Vellem, Vuyani. "Epistemological Dialogue as Prophetic: A Black Theological Perspecive on the Land Issue." *Scriptura* 115/1 (2016) 1–11. https://scriptura.journals.ac.za/pub/article/view/1201.

Bibliography

Adebayo, Adekeye. *The Curse of Berlin: Africa after the Cold War*. London: Hurst, 2010.

Aidele, P. Onyemechi. *The Popes, the Catholic Church and the Transatlantic Enslavement of Black Africans 1418–1839*. Hildesheim: Olms, 2017.

Albertz, Rainer. *Israel in Exile: The History and Literature of the Sixth Century*. Studies in Biblical Literature 3. Atlanta: Society of Biblical Literature, 2003.

African National Congress. "Report of the 54th National Conference" (2018). https://www.polity.org.za/article/54th-national-conference-report-and-resolutions-2018-03-26.

Baartman, Ernest N. "The Significance of the Development of Black Consciousness for the Church." *Journal of Theology for Southern Africa* 2 (1973) 18–22.

Bax, Douglas. "The Bible and Apartheid 2." In *Apartheid Is a Heresy*, edited by John W. de Gruchy and Charles Villa-Vicencio, 112–43. Grand Rapids: Eerdmans, 1983.

———. *A Different Gospel: A Critique of the Theology behind Apartheid*. Johannesburg: Presbyterian Church of Southern Africa, 1981.

Blenkinsopp, Joseph. "Was the Pentateuch the Civic and Religious Constitution of the Jewish Ethnos in the Persian Period?" In *Persia and Torah: The Theory of Imperial Authorization of the Pentateuch*, edited by James W. Watts, 41–62. SBL Symposium Series 17. Atlanta: Society of Biblical Literature, 2001.

Blum, Erhard. *Studien zur Komposition des Pentateuch*. Beihefte zur Zeitschrift für die alttestamentliche Wissenschaft 189. Berlin: de Gruyter, 1990.

Boesak, Allan. *Farewell to Innocence: A Socio-Ethical Study on Black Theology and Black Power*. 1976. Reprinted, Eugene, OR: Wipf & Stock, 2015.

Bosman, Hendrik. "The 'Jerusalemgangers' as an Illustration of Resistance against the British Empire and Nineteenth Century Biblical Interpretation in Southern Africa." In *In the Name of God: The Bible in the Colonial Discourse of Empire*, edited by C. L. Crouch and Jonathan Stökl, 151–62. Biblical Interpretation Series 126. Leiden: Brill, 2014.

Braun, Lindsay F. "The Returns of the King: The Case of Mphephu and Western Venda, 1899–1904." *Journal of Southern African Studies* 39 (2013) 271–91.

Brett, Mark G. "Reading the Bible in the Context of Methodological Pluralism: The Undermining of Ethnic Pluralism in Genesis." In *Rethinking Contexts, Rereading Texts: Contributions from the Social Sciences to Biblical Interpretation*, edited by M. Daniel Carroll R., 48–74. Journal for the Study of the Old Testament Supplement Series 299. Sheffield: Sheffield Academic, 2000.

Brueggemann, Walter. *The Land: Place as Gift, Promise, and Challenge in Biblical Faith*. Philadelphia: Fortress, 1977.

Charles, Mark. "The Doctrine of Discovery, War, and the Myth of America." *Leaven* 24/3 (2016) 148–54.

Chipanga, C., and Mude Torque. "Sanctions against Zimbabwe Were Unsuccessful and Harmful." In *Economic Sanctions*, edited by K. L. Heitkamp, 74–81. New York: Greenhaven, 2019.

Cone, James H. *A Black Theology of Liberation: Twentieth Anniversary Edition*. Maryknoll, NY: Orbis, 1990.

———. *God of the Oppressed*. New York: Seabury, 1975.

Crüsemann, F. "Le Pentateuque, une Tora: Prolégomènes et interpretation de sa forme finale." In *Le Pentateuque en question*, edited by Albert de Pury et al., 339–60. 2nd ed. Le Monde de la Bible 19. Geneva: Labor et Fides, 1989.

Day, David. *Conquest: How Societies Overwhelm Others.* Oxford: Oxford University Press, 2008.

Degenaar, Johannes. "Philosophical Roots of Nationalism." In *Church and Nationalism in South Africa,* edited by Theo Sundermeier, 11–39. Johannesburg: Ravan, 1975.

De Gruchy, John W. "Political Landmarks and the Response of Churches in South Africa." *Journal of Theology for Southern Africa* 118 (2004) 3–26.

———. *The Church Struggle in South Africa.* Cape Town: David Phillip, 1979.

Dozeman, Thomas B., Thomas Römer, and Konrad Schmid, eds. *Pentatuech, Hexateuch, or Enneateuch? Identifying Literary Works in Genesis through Kings.* Ancient Israel and Its Literature 8. Atlanta: Society of Biblical Literature, 2011.

Dube, Musa. "Jesse Mugambi Is Calling Us to Move from Liberation to Reconstruction! A Postcolonial Feminist Response." Paper delivered at a symposium at the University of South Africa, 2002.

Dutch Reformed Church. *Human Relations and the South African Scene in the Light of Scripture.* Cape Town: Dutch Reformed Church, 1976.

———. *Reply of the Dutch Reformed Church to the Report of the Reformed Churches in the Netherlands in Connection with the Programme to Combat Racism.* Cape Town: D. R. Church, 1976.

Du Toit, André. "Captive to the Nationalist Paradigm: Prof F. A. van Jaarsveld and the Historical Evidence for the Afrikaner's Ideas on His Calling and Mission." *South African Historical Journal* 16 (1984) 49–80.

———. "No Chosen People: The Myth of the Calvinist Origins of Afrikaner Nationalism and Racial Ideology." *American Historical Review* 88 (1983) 920–52. https://www.jstor.org/stable/1874025.

Dwane, Sigqibo. "Christology and Liberation." *Journal of Theology in Southern Africa* 35 (1981) 29–37.

Fanon, Frantz. *Black Skins, White Masks.* Translated by C. L. Markmann. London: Pluto, 2008.

Farisani, Elelwani. "Black Biblical Hermeneutics and Ideologically Aware Reading of Texts." *Scriptura* 105 (2010) 507–18.

———. "The Use of Ezra–Nehemiah in a Quest for an African Theology of Reconstruction. *Journal of Theology for Southern Africa* 116 (2003) 27–50.

———. "The Ideologically Biased Use of Ezra–Nehemiah in a Quest for an African Theology of Reconstruction." *Old Testament Essays* 15 (2002) 628–46.

Frei, Peter. "Persian Imperial Authorization: A Summary." In *Persia and Torah: The Theory of Imperial Authorization of the Pentateuch,* edited by James W. Watts, 5–40. SBL Symposium Series 17. Atlanta: Society of Biblical Literature, 2001.

———. "Die Persische Reichsautorisation: Ein Überblick." *Zeitschrift für altorientalische und biblische Rechtsgeschichte* 1 (1995) 1–35.

Giliomee, Hermann B. *The Afrikaners: Biography of a People.* Cape Town: Tafelberg, 2003.

Giliomee, Hermann B., and Bernard Mbenga. *New History of South Africa.* Cape Town: Tafelberg, 2007.

Green, Barbara. "Great Trek and Long Walk: Readings of a Biblical Symbol." *Biblical Interpretation* 7 (1999) 272–300.

Habel, Norman C. *The Land Is Mine: Six Biblical Land Ideologies.* Overtures to Biblical Theology. Minneapolis: Fortress, 1995.

Hagedorn, Anselm C. "Persia and Torah: The Theory of Imperial Authorization of the Pentateuch." *Biblical Interpretation* 13 (2005) 67–69.

Johnson, Willa M. 2011. *The Holy Seed Has Been Defiled. The Interethnic Marriage Dilemma in Ezra 9–10*. Hebrew Bible Monographs 33. Sheffield: Sheffield Phoenix, 2011.

Khapoya, Vincent B. *The African Experience: An Introduction*, 4th ed. Upper Saddle River, NJ: Pearson, 2013.

Kiefer, Jörn. *Exil und Diaspora: Begrifflichkeit und Deutungen im antiken Judentum und in der hebräischen Bibel*. Leipzig: Evangelische Verlagsanstalt, 2005.

Kiogora, Timothy G. "Black Hermeneutics." In *Initiation into Theology: The Rich Variety of Theology and Hermeneutics*, edited by S. Maimela and A. König, 337–47. Pretoria: JL van Schaik, 1998.

Kinghorn, J., edited. *Die NG Kerk en Apartheid*. Johannesburg: Macmillan, 1986.

Knoppers, Gary N. "An Achaemenid Imperial Authorization of Torah in Yehud?" In *Persia and Torah: The Theory of Imperial Authorization of the Pentateuch*, edited by James W. Watts, 115–35. SBL Symposium Series 17. Atlanta: Society of Biblical Literature, 2001.

Knoppers, Gary N., and Bernard M. Levinson, eds. *The Pentateuch as Torah: New Models for Understanding Its Promulgation and Acceptance*. Winona Lake, IN: Eisenbrauns, 2007.

Kratz, Reinhard G. "The Pentateuch in Current Research: Consensus and Debate." In *The Pentateuch: International Perspectives on Current Research*, edited by Thomas B. Dozeman, translated by A. C. Hagedorn, 31–61. Forschungen zum Alten Testament 78. Tübingen: Mohr Siebeck, 2011.

Kretzshmar, Louise. *The Voice of Black Theology in South Africa*. Johannesburg: Raven, 1986.

Landman, W. A. *A Plea for Understanding: A Reply to the Reformed Church in America*. Cape Town: D. R., 1968.

Maimela, Simon. "Black Theology." In *Initiation into Theology: The Rich Variety of Theology and Hermeneutics*, edited by S. Maimela and A. König, 111–19. Pretoria: JL van Schaik, 1998.

Maluleke, Tinyiko S. "Black Theology as Public Discourse." In *Constructing a Language of Religion in Public Life: Multi-Event 1999 Academic Workshop Papers*, edited by James R. Cochrane, 60–62. Cape Town: University of Cape Town, 1998.

———. "Black and African Theologies in the New World Order: A Time to Drink from Our Own Wells." *Journal of Theology for Southern Africa* 96 (1996) 3–19.

Mamdani, Mahmood. *When Victims Become Killers: Colonialism, Nativism, and the Genocide in Rwanda*. Princeton: Princeton University, 2001.

Matondi, Prosper B. *Zimbabwe's Fast Track Land Reform*. London: Zed, 2012.

Miller, Robert J. "The Doctrine of Discovery." In *Discovering Indigenous Lands: The Doctrine of Discovery in the English Colonies*, edited by Robert J. Miller, Jacinta Ruru, Larissa Behrendt, and Tracey Lindberg. Oxford: Oxford University, 2010.

Mkodzongi, G., and Lawrence Peter. "The Fast Track Land Reform and Agrarian Change in Zimbabwe." *Review of African Political Economy* 46/159 (2019) 1–13. https://www.tandfonline.com/doi/full/10.1080/03056244.2019.1622210.

Mofokeng, Takatso A. "Black Christians, the Bible and Liberation." *Journal of Black Theology* 2 (1988) 34–42.

———. "Land Is Our Mother: A Black Theology of Land." In *An African Challenge to the Church in the Twenty-First Century*, edited by M. Guma and A. L. Milton, 42–56. Cape Town: Salty Print, 1997.

Mosala, Itumeleng. "Land, Class and the Bible in South Africa Today." *Journal of Black Theology in South Africa* 5/2 (1991) 40–45.
————. *Biblical Hermeneutics and Black Theology in South Africa*. Grand Rapids: Eerdmans, 1989.
Moyo, Sam. "Changing Agrarian Relations after Redistributive Land Reform in Zimbabwe." *Journal of Peasant Studies* 38 (5) 939–66. https://www.tandfonline.com/doi/full/10.1080/03066150.2011.634971.
Mugambi, Jesse N. K. *Christian Theology and Social Reconstruction*. Nairobi: Acton, 2003.
————. *From Liberation to Reconstruction: African Christian Theology after the Cold War*. Nairobi: EAEP, 1995.
————. "The Future of the Church and the Church of the Future in Africa." In *The Church of Africa: Towards a Theology of Reconstruction*, edited by J. B. Chipenda, A. Karamaga, J. N. K. Mugambi, and C. K. Omari. Nairobi: AACC, 1991.
————. "Religion and Social Reconstruction in Post-Colonial Africa." In *Church-State Relations: A Challenge for African Christianity*, edited by J. N. K. Mugambi and F. Kürshcner-Pelkmann. Nairobi: Acton, 2004.
Otto, Eckart. "Forschungen zum Nachpriesterschriftlichen Pentateuch." *Theologische Rundschau* 67 (2002) 125–55.
Parratt, John. "The Marxist Trend in Recent South African Black Theology: Is Dialogue Possible?" *Mission Studies* 6/2 (1989) 77–86.
Pearce, Fred. *The Land Grabbers: The New Fight Over Who Owns the Earth*. Boston: Beacon, 2012.
Petersen, Robin. "Towards a South African Theology of Non-Racialism." *Journal of Theology for Southern Africa* 77 (1991) 18–26.
Pitkänen, Pekka. "Pentateuch–Joshua: A Settler-Colonial Document of a Supplanting Society." *Settler Colonial Studies* 4 (2014) 245–76.
Römer, Thomas. "How Many Books (Teuchs): Pentateuch, Hexateuch, or Ennaeteuch?" In *Pentateuch, Hexateuch, or Ennaeuteuch: Identifying Literary Works in Genesis through Kings*, edited by T. B. Dozeman, 25–42. Ancient Israel and Its Literature 8. Atlanta: Society of Biblical Literature, 2011.
Schmid, Konrad. *Genesis and the Moses Story: Israel's Dual Origins in the Hebrew Bible*. Winona Lake, IN: Eisenbrauns, 2010.
————. "The Late Persian Formation of the Torah: Observations on Deuteronomy 34." In *Judah and the Judeans in the Fourth Century B.C.E.*, edited by O. Lipschits, G. N. Knoppers and R. Albertz, 237–51. Winona Lake, In: Eisenbrauns, 2007.
Ska, Jean-Louis. *Introduction to Reading the Pentateuch*. Winona Lake, IN: Eisenbrauns, 2006.
West, Gerald O. *The Academy of the Poor: Towards a Dialogical Reading of the Bible*. 1999. Reprint, Pietermaritzburg: Cluster, 2008.
————. *Biblical Hermeneutics of Liberation: Modes of Reading the Bible in the South African Context*. Second revised edition. Pietermaritzburg: Cluster Publications, 1995.
————. "Negotiating with 'the White Man's Book': Early Foundations for Liberation Hermeneutics in Southern Africa." In *African Theology Today*, vol. 1, edited by E. M. Katongole, 23–56. Scranton: University of Scranton Press, 2002.
Tutu, Desmond M. *Hope and Suffering: Sermons and Speeches*. Johannesburg: Skotaville, 1983.

———. "The Theology of Liberation in Africa." In *African Theology en Route: Pan African Conference of Third World Theologians, Accra, Ghana, 1977*, edited by Kofi Appiah-Kubi and Sergio Torres, 162–68. Maryknoll, NY: Orbis, 1979.

Villa-Vicencio, Charles. "Keeping the Revolution Human: Religion and Reconstruction." *Journal for the Study of Religion* 6/2 (1993) 49–68.

Vellem, Vuyani S. "Ideology and Spirituality: A Critique of Villa-Vicencio's Project of Reconstruction." *Scriptura* 105 (2010) 547–58.

Veracini, Lorenzo. *Settler Colonialism: A Theoretical Overview*. New York: Palgrave, 2010.

Vorster, Willem. "The Bible and Apartheid 1." In *Apartheid Is a Heresy*, edited by John W. de Gruchy and Charles Villa-Vicencio, 94–111. Grand Rapids: Eerdmans, 1983.

Wöhrle, Jakob. "The Un-Empty Land: The Concept of Exile and Land in P." In *The Concept of Exile in Ancient Israel and Its Historical Contexts*, edited by Ehud Ben Zvi and Christoph Levin, 189–206. Beihefte zur Zeitschrift fur die alttestamentliche Wissenschaft 404. Berlin: de Gruyter, 2010.

Watts, James W., ed. *Persia and Torah: The Theory of Imperial Authorization of the Pentateuch*. SBL Symposium Series 17. Atlanta: Society of Biblical Literature, 2001.

Wolfe, Patrick. "Settler Colonialism and the Elimination of the Native." *Journal of Genocide Research* 8 (2006) 387–409.

———. "Structure and Event: Settler Colonialism, Time, and the Question of Genocide." In *Empire, Colony, Genocide: Conquest, Occupation, and Subaltern Resistance in World History*, edited by A Dirk Moses, 102–32. Studies on War and Genocide 12. New York: Berghahn, 2010.

Wright, Christopher J. H. *God's People in God's Land: Family, Land, and Property in the Old Testament*. Grand Rapids: Eerdmans, 1990.

Conclusion

Theologies of Land

Contested Land, Spatial Justice,
and Covenantal Identity

K. K. Yeo

A Theological Autobiography

"Where is home?" I'm often asked. The reply, "I don't know." Or, "Nowhere and everywhere."

Being a son of the Chinese diaspora, my life has been a journey through a *mixed and messy* space. I was born and raised in a small coastal town called Kuching at the northwestern tip of Borneo, the third-largest island on earth. The South China Sea allowed my father and grandfather to flee the civil war in China. They arrived in Kuching on a cargo ship on July 7, 1937, the day the Imperial Japanese Army invaded Beijing—the invasion that marked the start of the Second Sino-Japanese War. Since the 1900s my family in China had been living in a decimated land and deteriorating landscape because of war. Thinking Borneo to be a sanctuary, if not a refuge, my parents lived through the Japanese occupation until September 2, 1945. The Japanese empire forced the local population to learn the Japanese language; the produce of their land, crops, and especially the livestock were to be levied to support the Japanese army. My young mind detested the stories of brutality and prejudice of the Japanese army that our parents told my siblings and me. Memories of violence, occupation, assimilation on the land tainted my traumatic consciousness. From a young age, I discovered that "space is political and ideological."[1] Therefore, territory is frequently contested and this results in a groaning of the "blue planet" and cries of its peoples for freedom and dignity.

From 1840 until 1963, before the independence of Malaysia, Northern Borneo was colonized by the British Empire (and Southern Borneo of Indonesia by the Dutch). In a relatively peaceful time, cultural adaptation, constant negotiation with local multi-culturalism, and the soft colonization program of the Empire, then Commonwealth, "trained" my family to survive as a hybridized entity. All my siblings attended Chinese primary school, and most of us were sent to English-medium secondary schools set up by Christian missionaries. I became a Christian in secondary school yet was ever confounded by my evolving identity as I faced the vicissitudes of a life in a world devoid of justice and dignity. The changing terrain around me prompted me to explore who and whose I was in terms of my familial, cultural, national, and theological identities.

After Malaysia's independence from the British, I observed that "the colonized" became "the colonizers" as the Malays made an exclusive claim to be the "princes of the soil" (*bumiputra*). The binary language of colonizer/colonized is hardly accurate enough to describe the complex and fluid world we live in—the colonizers are not just in "the West," they are also in the East and South, and even among our own people (internal and intercolonialisms), as power disguises itself as truth. The previously colonized immigrant communities (Chinese and Indian) not only contributed to the welfare of the sovereign territory but also robbed the land of its natural resources. The timber industry, mostly owned by the new immigrant communities, was booming, resulting in deforestation and severe flooding, not to mention ruining the livelihood of many people whose living depended on the land. Entrepreneurs, local and foreign, moved in and converted paddy fields to oil palm plantations for biofuel profits. Under the guise of development and modernization, the new immigrants bled the earth and destroyed the basic sustenance of the people. The ecology of Borneo changed, and the poor became poorer. Only when I pursued theological study twenty years later did I realize how irresponsible and abusive we all are to the land, its people, and its non-human creatures. Unfortunately, much of the Christian preaching and teaching I received before my theological training was unconscious of the fact that the perpetrators were either ignorant of eco-justice and economic and political

1. Soja, *Postmodern Geographies*, 80.

hegemony, or they inadvertently continued the devastation of the land. I began to connect the dots, seeing the link between natural disasters such as tsunamis and forest fires and the greedy machinery of obsessive capitalism. I also wonder if the "homelessness" of my parents because of war in China gave them the right to buy and own land in Borneo? Have they encroached on others' land? Are not the Indigenous Peoples the original and perpetual owners of the land? And are the Malays the "first" peoples in Borneo and Malaysia who then can make historical claim to the land? My "homeless" identity was exacerbated when schoolmates and strangers mocked me, "Go back to China!"

Throughout my life, my "nomadic consciousness" of *space* in terms of connection has been shaped by the givenness of distance and the yearning for communication and communion. "Self-isolation" and "social distancing" were inevitable realities during the Great Leap Forward (1958–1962) and the Great Proletarian Cultural Revolution (1966–1976) in China, when families in Malaysia were cut off from those in China. From a young age, I loved listening to a shortwave radio for "distant closeness" with news of how my family in China was doing. It was a shocking awakening after 1976 when China opened its gates and I discovered that most news reports were propaganda masquerading in nationalistic tone. I learned that millions suffered in these periods that were rightly judged as a "great leap backward" and a time of "cultural destruction."[2] Disastrous policies of land reform and redistribution, made worse by party-state mismanagement, brought about famine in addition to the systematic torture of landlords and dissidents. Frank Dikötter's research shows that between 1958 and 1962 at least 40 million died of starvation and mass killings.[3] Fast forward to the last twenty years when I have lived in Beijing under its heavy smog and then, since December 2019, we all are living in the nightmare of the COVID-19 pandemic. The modern BC (Before Coronavirus) world evidently did not learn the lesson of SARS seventeen years prior, when health professionals in 2003 warned of the habit of consuming "exotic" animals, not to mention the wildlife trafficking such as rhinos and pangolins. Humanity continued to be anthropocentric and dominating in "raping the land" (to use ecofeminist language) and its people and all the creatures, thus making the land and its people infected with "novel" virus. We continued to

2. See Yeo, *Chairman Mao Meets the Apostle Paul*, 139–62, 191–212.
3. Dikötter, *Mao's Great Famine*, 8.

make the earth homelessness and "roaring" in protest?[4] The discussion regarding the "jump" of the virus from bats to human will continue, but the pandemic raises for us ancient theological questions already found in the Bible regarding the relevance of "food laws" or not, the humility to respect "chaos" (as in the metaphor of "the Sea") and our inability to "rid the evil" (only empire militarism has such arrogance and ingorance), as well as the wisdom not to "conquer the land." I agree with Arundhati Roy, who wrote a reflection on the COVID-19 pandemic, "Coronavirus has made the mighty kneel and brought the world to a halt like nothing else could. . . . [I]n the midst of this terrible despair, it offers us a chance to rethink the doomsday machine we have built for ourselves."[5]

I tell my story briefly, hoping to include a voice from that region called Asia—the most iridescent continent of expansive geographic space with a myriad of cultures. But more importantly, I hope to dialogue with the four contributors, making the point that happenings in other regions are not disconnected from the rest of us. There are two theological purposes for this autobiography.[6] Firstly, it hints at the intricate relationship among land(scape), migration, and identity—the three mega-themes this series (*Crosscurrents in Majority World and Minority Theology*; CMWMT) wants to explore in individual volumes—and yet acknowledges the ways these three topics inevitably crisscross each other.[7] Secondly, it points to the complex issues arising out of political domination and humanity's abuse of land, consequently creating unjust space, homelessness of people, and a broken landscape of God's creation. Human greed and land grabs result in not only religious wars and ethnic cleansing but also environmental degradation that exasperates epidemic outbreaks, typhoons and tornados.

4. Griffin, *Woman and Nature*, 122, 171.

5. Roy, "The Pandemic Is a Portal." He continues, "Historically, pandemics have forced humans to break with the past and imagine their world anew. This one is no different. It is a portal, a gateway between one world and the next. We can choose to walk through it, dragging the carcasses of our prejudice and hatred, our avarice, our data banks and dead ideas, our dead rivers and smoky skies behind us. Or we can walk through lightly, with little luggage, ready to imagine another world. And ready to fight for it."

6. I wrote about this experience and offered a theological reflection in my three books: *Chairman Mao Meets the Apostle Paul*; *Musing with Confucius and Paul*; and *Eve, Gaia and God*.

7. See Dawson and Rapport edited, *Migrants of Identity*.

Our Polyvalent Conferencing

The contributors to this volume invite readers to engage with their essays, while readers also are encouraged to take their social locations and embodied space seriously. Personal narrative has an eccentric effect on the way we, the global church, read the Bible toward the flourishing of life. We were quickly aware at our San Diego conference in November 2019 that there is no one theology of land but only *theologies* of land because each contributor's context or embodiment is so different from another. Yet, there are many underlying themes that intersect and enlighten each other's contexts. Theologies and biblical interpretations of the Majority World and minoritized communities are highlighted in this series because their voices are often missing or ignored by the global church, especially churches in the Global North. The theological loci that the Majority World and minoritized communities aspire beyond traditional reflections include: the reciprocity of covenant in the creation story; predatory ideology of colonizing theology in making Indigenous Peoples landless; the role of the Bible in reconstruction theology for the Indigenous Peoples to re-possess the land; the ways to overcome the Zionist theological legitimacy in colonizing Palestine, or to overcome biblical interpretation that harms the land and its peoples. Compared with the theologies traditionally done by the North Atlantic region, Majority World and minoritized communities offer "more sociopolitical readings of biblical [texts and life contexts], . . . more cross-culturally linguistically but also contextually because of their rich traditions, . . . [and more] actively engaging with public life rather than submit to a Christian secular divide that sees piety as purely personal."[8]

Before bringing the four contributors to a conference table to discuss critical issues shared by the four essays, allow me to reintroduce them as necessary interlocutors and people of their varied contexts. Each of them has a background that is hybridized and unique. The contributor of the third essay is Rev. Dr. Danny Zacharias, a Cree-Anishinaabe and Austrian man from Treaty One territory in Manitoba, Canada. He is an associate professor of New Testament Studies at Acadia Divinity College in Nova Scotia, located in the ancestral and unceded territory of the Mi'kmaq peoples, and is ordained with the Convention of the Atlantic Baptist Churches. He also serves as a faculty member with *NAIITS: An Indigenous Learning Community*. Zacharias writes of his essay, "Despite common Christian

8. Yeo, "Biblical Interpretation in the Majority World," 169.

discourse on environmental stewardship and creation care, my essay is a careful reading of the biblical text from an intercultural framework. It shows that humanity is part of the community of creation, not above it. Furthermore, we are placed into a relationship of reciprocity with the land, a relationship in which we are the ones cared for. The biblical portrait of our relationship with land is one of inter-dependence and inter-relatedness. This essay's exegetical work has important theological implications for building theologies of land and place."[9]

The contributor of the first essay is the Rev. Dr. Mitri Raheb, founder and president of Dar al-Kalima University College of Arts and Culture in Bethlehem, Palestine. He was previously a long-time senior pastor of Christmas Lutheran Church at Bethlehem. Raheb summarizes the intention of his essay: "The land theology was used to colonize land all over the world. This is true also for Palestine. Christian Zionist theologies, as well as liberal Zionist theologies, provided the State of Israel with a theological legitimacy to colonize Palestine. However, several new voices have emerged in the last thirty years that have read the Bible in a de-colonial or post-colonial perspective, including many Palestinian and several Jewish voices. The main focus of the Bible is liberation and not colonization."

Born in Honduras, our contributor of the second essay is Rev. Dr. García-Johnson, an ordained minister with American Baptist Churches, USA. He is assistant provost and associate professor of Theology and Latino/a Studies at Fuller Theological Seminary, California. García-Johnson whets our appetite with the following remarks regarding his essay, "The social imaginary of Europeans was transformed when they discovered the route to the Atlantic and came to experience the vastness and diversity of the lands and peoples of the Americas (*Anáhuac, Tahuantinsuyu,* and *'Ayiti*). Concretely, local European kings and kingdoms became global landlords, and local indigenous kingdoms and civilizations became a global labor force and landless peoples. In one phrase: *the shape of the theology of the land in the Americas is until today a theology of the landlords and the landless.*"

The fourth contributor is Dr. Huli Ramantswana, associate professor at the University of South Africa. His works champion the importance of

9. Those quotations without page numbers cited throughout this essay are either contributors' written responses or oral exchanges at the San Diego conference in November 2019. All four contributors have read this essay and approved their own quotations used in it. My preference is to use direct speech to preserve the *polyvalent* conferencing and its process, rather than the indirect speech of giving my perspective and rendering their voices in *my* words.

reading the Bible by comparing the knowledge systems and life experience of the African context with the knowledge systems and life experience of the text. Ramantswana gives an abstract of his essay, "On one hand, the essay reflects on land issues, as the first section highlights the problem of the Bible as a colonial instrument for dispossessing African people of their land and, on the other hand, it points to the use of the Bible by Africans in getting their land back. The second section focuses on 'reconstruction theology,' in contrast to 'Black Theology of liberation,' considering the demise of colonialism. The third section gives attention to the motif of the promised land as projected in the Hexateuch from a decolonial perspective. The paper argues for a decolonial theology of land that wrestles with the dynamics of settler colonialism."

To guide us through these theologies of land of minoritized communities and the Majority World, the following three sections take up a few critical questions that emerged in the four essays and the San Diego conference Gene Green and I organized.

Theology and Its Ground:
Materiality of Theology and Life's Context

1. Why do theologies of land matter to you or your people?

All four essays affirm adamantly that land matters to them because who they are is based substantially on the land. The word "land" is a metaphor, meaning "it is, it is not, it is more (than)" the land. Land matters because it is the *ground* for one's existence, it is the *home* of residence, and it is the *materiality* of one's identity. Zacharias points to the materiality of his indigenous theology, "Many Indigenous peoples live out their theologies of land. It is much more a practice than an articulated belief system. The articulation of these theologies is in some sense a capitulation to Western abstraction. These descriptions matter because Indigenous peoples recognize themselves as part of the community of creation."

In these essays "land" is used as a dynamic idiom that points to the nexus, which expands and connects to one's history, imagination, and identity. "Land" is generative language that signifies "landscape" which, in Krista Comer's words, "[is not] an empty field of vision (the premise of perceptual geography) but rather a brimming-full social topography that creates and enacts the various cultural assumptions and power struggles of the age."[10] In this essay, as well as in the other four essays, land and landscape are used interchangeably to make sense of one's identity in the dynamic flow of history and community life. Kirby Farrell explains this usage well: "landscape is a form of psychic topography, and history is a record of attempts not just to own land, but to identify with it. Land is 'ground' (*Grund* and *Boden*), the foundation of life."[11] In that regard, García-Johnson is forthright about his work on "the Transamerican theology," in which he intends to give voice to "the native peoples of the conquered land" thereby "re-traditioning the theology of the land with indigenous content for them. The majority of people are the *landless* and very few the *landlords*; they are (and have been) in migration crisis–believers seeking for land and trapped in hopeless neoliberal circuits."

Given that theology is "embodied" (enfleshed or incarnational), conflict over land or territory results in concrete devastation of the identity of the Indigenous Peoples, on their lives, or on their dignity. Hearing every story retold by the four scholars regarding land loss or landlessness in the contexts of land conquest and land grabs, I reheard my own story. Ultimately, the art of storytelling raises a question about "who and whose I am?" Am I Chinese and how do I affiliate with China (and which China?), and/or with Malaysia? This "ethnic correlation" is obvious for some, such as dominant groups—Englishmen and England, or Scots and Scotland. But to define the ethnic correlation is polemical for many, especially Indigenous Peoples or marginal groups such as, Balkans, Albanians,[12] Palestinians, Latinx, and black South Africans, or people living in "out of place" with their culturally significant lands amidst territorial divisions and conflicts. Land matters.

2. How do you view the relationship between land and spirituality? In what sense is land "holy"?

Landscape and sacred space are intertwined. Semantics suggests that words such as "Eden," "Jerusalem," "Bethlehem," and "Palestine" refer not so much to lands but to *symbolic landscapes* charged with transcendent significance; similarly, signifiers such as "Manitoba," "Borneo," and "South Africa" do as well. J. Cornelis de Vos, a professor at the University

---

10. Comer, *Landscapes of the New West*, 13.

11. Farrell, "Eschatological Landscape," 118.

12. Saltman, "Introduction," 3.

of Münster, explains how Joshua 13–19 has an understanding of land distribution *among the twelve tribes* that is connected to the idea of proximity to the divine presence, as he visualized in the understanding of "graded holiness."[13] But note that in a lot of traditional scholarship of the Old Testament, Indigenous groups and settled communities are invisible (see also Raheb's essay). Who are the non-Jewish groups, such as the Arabs, in the Old Testament? Here I rely on Palestinian scholars or scholars who work on Palestinian theology,[14] e.g., to identify Geshem (or Gashmu) the Arab (Neh 2:19, 6:1) in the biblical text. I also have paid attention to "non-Israelites" in the Bible, those who are people of God without being proselytized as Jews or in Jewish cultures: 1) Melchizedek of Salem (Gen 14:18; Ps 110:4; Heb 5:6–20, 7:1–17); 2) Job in the land of Uz (Job; Jas 5:11); 3) Araunah, the Jebusite king (2 Sam 24:16–24), also called Ornan (2 Chron 21), a priest who offered King David the "temple mount" (as it was called later on, or the ground of Mt. Zion), and David knew better not to "grab" the land but paid for it; 4) Rahab (Josh 2; Heb 11:31; Jas 2:25); 5) Uriah the Hittite (husband of Bathsheba, 2 Sam 11; Matt 1:6); and 6) the Queen of Sheba (1 Kgs 10); 7), Moses' Cushite wife (Num 12:1); etc. Is the "promise of land" not given to these "non-Israelites"? Does the Old Testament suggest that land is not relevant or less relevant to the "non-Israelites" because God calls people who are not "people of the land"?

In terms of the sacredness of land, Zacharias shares with us the holistic understanding of his people, "Understanding that the land is sacred is one of the key components of understanding many Indigenous theologies of land. It is key because it is part of deconstructing the colonializing powers, objectified view of creation. To be sacred is to be set apart, recognized, and honored for a particular purpose given by the Creator. The land holds primacy of place as sacred given mother earth's role in sustaining all of life on earth. Because the Creator's design is for the land to be the liminal space where we continue to receive blessing, it only makes sense that our spirituality, holistically understood, would be tied to the land."

Likewise, Ramanstwana draws on the Indigenous South African understanding on the nature of "a sacred place": "The land is a sacred place we share with other forms of nature. The sacredness of the land was in the

13. de Vos, "'Holy Land' in Joshua 18:1–10," 72.

14. Such as Ateek, *Justice and Only Justice*; Wagner, *Dying in the Land of Promise*; Isaac, *From Land to Lands,* and the works of Katanacho (*The Land of Christ*) and Raheb (*I Am a Palestinian Christian*).

living in harmony with other forms of nature; it is no wonder that: 1) in our totems, we use animal names; 2) we refer to sacred spaces as '*zwifho*' or '*zwifhoni*' [sacred natural site]; and 3) many people wish to be buried in their home place, which is considered sacred. There are many *vhaVenḓa* people who, although they live and work in the cities, still prefer to be buried in the Venda area where they grew up."

It seems to me that all four contributors have a common purpose in their writings of examining "how identities emerge socially and spatially, how just and unjust geographies are formed and challenged, and how acts of writing [such as this book] . . . might contribute towards what Soja terms 'spatial justice.'"[15]

Biblical Theology and Its Texts

3. What is the role of the Bible in the theologies of land? Is the problem regarding the land issue your people faced caused by misinterpretation of the Bible (and theology) and/or the Bible itself, which contains some "toxic" texts?

This is a difficult question for many of us, partly because our contexts and our reception of the Bible are different, and we are encountering it at different phases. The most forceful response to this question comes from Raheb, perhaps because of the direct implication of the historical land in the Bible and the "same" physical land in which Palestinians live today. Raheb's essay will jolt many readers out of their misinterpretation of the Bible to oppress the weak and the poor. He writes, "Theology of land matters to us as Palestinians because of the Zionist colonization of our land Palestine and the use of the Bible to legitimize such colonization. Theology is here part of the problem. The Bible contains some toxic texts, like the book of Joshua that *literally* speaks of an ethnic cleansing. On the other hand, the Bible is being weaponized by people in power for their colonization projects. Yet, the Bible was intended as a book of the occupied to give them a sense of belonging to the land and as a promise for liberation and peace."

In the South African context, the *mixed role* of the Bible is also lifted up by Ramanstwana: "The Bible for the community of faith is not like any ordinary book; it is a book of faith. Therefore, for many in Africa, while

15. Berberich and Campbell, "Lines of Flight," 300. And see Sonja, *Seeking Spatial Justice*, 18.

the Bible was part and parcel of the colonizing instruments and a reminder of the loss of land, it also is regarded as a book that builds up the faith. However, accepting the Bible as a book of faith does not imply that readers should not be critical in their reading of the biblical texts." García-Johnson agrees with Raheb and Ramanstwana on the toxic readings of the biblical text by colonizers, in contrast to the liberating (political) readings of biblical texts by colonized readers.

Although these are challenging questions, there are at least two guiding principles all the authors forward in their essays that have helped them, and us, to use the Bible for liberation rather than oppression:

1. No book in the Bible is written as a universal handbook; thus, the historical contexts of the authors, of the redactors, and of the audience do matter.[16] Without context, then the myth of "a people without land" is matched to "a land without people,"[17] and such interpretation inadvertently sanctions the "genocide" of the settled communities in the name of the Holy Bible. On the one hand, the supersessionist or replacement Christian theology view of Jews' forfeiting the covenantal tie to the "Holy Land" because of their unfaithfulness to Yahweh (cf. Rom 3:1–18, 9:6–13) or their role in crucifying the Messiah Jesus (1 Thess 2:15) is a blatant misinterpretation.[18] On the other hand, it is incorrect to say the "Holy Land" belongs exclusively to the

---

16. Michaël van der Meer's thesis is that, "the Greek translator reduced the interest of the priestly redactors [of the book of Joshua] into a military stratagem of Joshua." One of best resources on the studies of conquest of people and occupation of land in the book of Joshua is, *The Land of Israel in Bible, History, and Theology*, edited van Ruiten and de Vos. Here the essay by van der Meer in this book is, "'Sound the Trumpet!' Redaction and Reception of Joshua 6:2–25," 40.

17. Zionism (secular or religious) is the belief that the land is promised by God for a people called Jews or Israel. Christian Zionism affirms that Jews or Israel have a unique place in God's election, salvation history, thus it is assumed that based on covenant (*berith*) and land (*eretz*) and the post-holocaust landlessness of this people, they can return to their "home"-land.

18. As expressed in another way by Pope Pius X to Theodor Herzl: "The Jews have not recognized our Lord, therefore we cannot recognize the Jewish people. . . . The Jewish faith was the foundation of our own, but it has been superseded by the teachings of Christ" (Patai, ed., *The Complete Diaries of Theodor Herzl* 4:1603). Taken from Cunningham, "A Catholic Theology of the Land?" 2. A dispensationalist approach to interpretation of the Bible, fueled with right-wing US politics, often has used the Bible to sanction political moves of supporting political (State of) Israel's aggression against Palestinians and the annexation of their lands. Walter Brueggemann calls "supersessionist" biblical interpretation "a historical absurdity and a theological scandal" (*Chosen?*, 28).

Jews because they are the "chosen people" with the eternal guarantee of land. The occupation of Palestinian land by the modern State of Israel, leaving so many Palestinian homeless, is hardly a correct response to anti-Judaism pogroms, and it is definitely not a correct interpretation of the Bible. Brueggemann observes that, "One can see at the edge of the Old Testament an inclusion of other peoples in the sphere of God's attentiveness, an inclusion that intends to mitigate any exclusionary claim by Israel."[19]

2. The Bible is a collection of diverse views, which are sometimes in disagreement with one another. Ramanstvana suggests, "The Bible is a site of plural voices that may not necessarily be reconciled with each other; therefore, listening to the plural voices is essential." Thus, scholars in this conference learn to cultivate the virtues of humility and mutual respect for the multiplicity of biblical interpretations. However, all interpreters are charged with an "ethic of biblical interpretation" that calls them to choose one appropriate interpretation for a particular context.[20]

Because of multiplicity, not just that of the biblical text and its context but also that of the readers of the Bible, there is no consensus about the next follow-up question, though all responses are potent and helpful.

4. Is your paper making an historical claim or a theological claim that the land belongs to Indigenous People only?

Zacharias is adamant about the "intrinsic right" and the "spiritual duty" of the Indigenous Peoples to the land, "Indigenous peoples belong to the land and have a spiritual duty to it. Peoples are entrusted to lands and are expected by the owner (God) to walk in a good way within the community of creation residing in that place. Those who have lived in lands for large spans of history and continue to be deeply connected spiritually to that place are those who have an intrinsic 'right' to the place."

Ramanstwana rejects the myth of "empty land." Instead, he uses the "claim of belonging" for his people: "The land in Southern Africa was not

---

19. See Brueggemann, *Chosen?*, 32; Brueggemann, *The Land*, 16–21.

20. See Daniel Patte on how to practice biblical studies that "accounts for the multiplicity of readings, related to the variety of contexts from which readers read." (Patte, *Ethics of Biblical Interpretation*, 29).

empty land up for grabs prior to the arrival of the colonialists. It is a colonial myth that our land was unoccupied. Therefore, the land belongs to those who were in the land prior to the arrival of European colonialists. For the Indigenous people, it is not just a matter of making a historical claim over the land; it is a claim of belonging. We belong to the African land. Theologically, the African land is a gift to the African people and, therefore, the Indigenous people have a responsibility over the land."

In agreement with Ramanstwana, Raheb responds, "The land belongs to the native people. This is a historic claim. But this claim meant to resist and prevent further colonization. The natives ask for justice. This is then a theological claim because the God of the Bible is the God of justice and liberation. Once justice is achieved, reconciliation and sharing of the land becomes possible."

My tentative position on this question has four points, which are based on a biblical theology of land. First, the "promise of land" in the OT is *mainly* about God's covenantal relationship with his peoples, *less* about land itself, and that is why the boundaries of "that" land "promised" are never clearly delineated but full of ambiguities.[21] Secondly, the biblical theology of land keeps pushing the "nationalistic" envelope of "chosen race" to expand God's faithfulness and people's *universal* reception of God's love and justice.[22] The Bible inveighs against God's peoples who mock his justice: "You shall not oppress a resident alien, you know the heart of an alien, for you were aliens in the land of Egypt" (Exod 23:9, NRSV).[23] Thirdly, a land, whether in Palestine or Borneo, is not a territorial guarantee to "first" residents (with a historical claim) or later migrants (with a political or moral claim). Rather, it is God's land given to the settled communities, who are to be as a custodian to the land with conditional promise and expected responsibility (to share and to take good care the land). The "conditional residence" is to live with God as "pilgrims"—pilgrims not in the sense of passing through the land but having a long view of God working in history as well as having a deep sense of connecting to the land—believing that God and his land will take care of

21. In a literal reading of "all nations on earth will be blessed" (Gen 26:4) in the Abrahamic covenant with God, then this boundary (in Gen 15:18 "from the river of Egypt to the great river, the Euphrates," including inclusive parts of modern day Egypt, Lebanon, Syria, Jordan, Iraq, and Saudi Arabia besides Palestine) is much bigger than "the land of Canaan" (Gen 12:5; Ps 105:6–11).

22. See Josh 1:7–8; Lev 20:22 ("You *shall keep all my statutes and ordinances, and observe* them, so that the land to which I bring you to settle in may not vomit you out.")

23. See also Exod 19:5; Isa 1:27, 5:16; 2 Chron 7:14; Prov 14:34; Ps 33:12.

them. Fourthly, *theological politics* of the land means that biblical theology guides political actions on the ground, rather than creating "facts on the ground" that go against biblical principles of justice, dignity, and love,[24] not to mention that they also break UN resolutions and international law on basic human rights. We just have heated dialogues.

When the four contributors were asked a follow-up question below, they all issued cautious responses:

> 5. *In your context, why is this statement helpful or not helpful:*
> *"The land belongs to God, not to people [we belong to the land] . . .*
> *therefore we need to speak of co-existence in sharing the land"?*

Our cultural assumption of land as private property, thus primary right, is a relatively modern idea. Early history of society considered land as common property; thus members of the community have equal rights to use the land for the common good. Privileged and powerful classes often seized the land and land conquest reduced the conquered into slaves—sometimes described by whitewashed words such as "servants" and "laborers." The feudal system basically tries to blend the common rights of real estate with the idea of exclusive property. Is it not a modern "feudal" system when my family in Malaysia has to pay for a piece of property (and in some instances a land ownership for lease of ninety-nine years only) and, in the case of US tax law, an annual property tax? All land in the People's Republic of China since 1949 is owned by collectivities or by the state, whose sovereignty and power are absolute. Therefore, land in China cannot be traded but can only be leased, while a property on the land can be transacted (property rights

24. See for examples (all biblical texts quoted in this essay are from NRSV): Gen 17:8 ("And I will give to you, and to your offspring after you, the land where you are now an alien, all the land of Canaan, for a perpetual holding; and I will be their God") has an expectation of responsibility in Gen 17:9–14 ("God said to Abraham, 'As for you, *you shall keep my covenant*, you and your offspring . . . This is my covenant, which *you shall keep* . . . .'"). The conditional clauses in Deuteronomy also are clear: "If the Lord your God enlarges your territory, . . . and he will give you all the land that he promised your ancestors to give you, *provided you diligently observe this entire commandment* that I command you today, by loving the Lord your God and walking always in his ways . . ." (Deut 19:8–9; also 28:1–3, 7, 10); Deut 16:20 ("*Justice, and only justice, you shall follow, so that* you may live and inherit the land that the Lord your God is giving you."); Deut 28:58 ("If you do *not diligently observe all* the words of this law that are written in this book, fearing this glorious and awesome name, the Lord your God, . . . you shall be plucked off the land that you are entering to possess.")

codified in the Property Law in 2007). So the answer to this question for people in China is given by the government, in the sense that the government determines which land may be shared by whom.

In his book *I Am a Palestinian Christian* published in 1995, Raheb understands the land as a gift of God to be shared: "The Land happens to be the homeland of two peoples. Each of them should understand this land to be a gift of God to be shared with the other. Peace and blessing on the land and on the two peoples will depend on this sharing."[25] At the San Diego conference in 2019, Raheb answered this question with "Palestine belongs to Palestinians," and qualified with two provocative rhetorical questions: "Who makes that statement? And how have the colonizers used this sort of statement to do injustice to Palestinians?"

Zacharias agrees with Raheb and surmises that, "Yes, we certainly do need to speak of co-existence and sharing. The problem is that this is most often framed by the colonial power. It becomes co-existence and sharing under their terms. A biblical theology of land, I believe, places the emphasis of authority on the original caretakers, not the invading settler." In the same view, García-Johnson echoes the concern of asymmetry of power, "Yes and no. How we see 'belonging to' changes the theological perspective. I would rather say, 'the land covenants with God on behalf of God's children.'"

Ramanstwana's view is to hold to both sharing and owning the land: "Theologically, the land belongs to God; however, biblically God did not make the earth his dwelling—his dwelling is in heaven (his throne room), the earth is human beings' dwelling. . . . The land/earth is a space to be shared. The willingness to share the land, however, does not obliterate the concept of land ownership."

The question of "co-existence" is important at least for raising two controversial questions: a) Who are the "Indigenous" or First Peoples in a given physical territory, when we know that war, intermarriage, and migration, among other factors, shift peoples across the same physical space? In a space where symmetry of power can be achieved (which is hardly possible), there is a heated discussion in our conference whether "the land is to be shared" and/or "the land belongs to the Indigenous Peoples." Even though biblical theology may affirm that since the land belongs to God, one might draw the conclusion that neither the settlers nor the Indigenous inhabitants can make exclusive claim of the territory. Yet, as indicated at the beginning of this section, property law of a nation state and diverse

25. Raheb, *I Am a Palestinian Christian*, 78.

understanding of land ownership by different cultures make the discussion of the exclusive claim of the territory challenging. Can a people-group establish and therefore claim to be the "first" people in the land historically, and therefore to own the land perpetually? Or should we acknowledge with Indigenous Peoples that they are the ones whose true identity is connected with a particular land and that on that land they serve as hosts? Being host of the land, will one want to practice the biblical admonition of "hospitality to strangers" (Heb 13:2), visitors, and migrants? We all agree that the "exclusive claim" of land does not mean condoning injustice inflicted upon the land and its peoples, remembering always the physical and spiritual sufferings inflicted by colonization on the land of others; b) In urban spaces of our world today, mobility of a mix of peoples is swift and frequent. Does this mean one's identity with land is secondary, if it is affiliated with one's identity at all? Has urban dwellers' sense of space shifted to different perspectives and media, including wide range of identity constructs with internet-technology devices to living with neighbors as strangers in high-rise condominiums? Much of this wants further discussion, but suffice to say that metropolitan living in a highly cross-cultural condition could be a humanizing project that promotes mutual respect, love, and justice—themes that are relevant to rural setting.

In sum, some of us would endorse the Kairos Palestinian Document saying: "We declare that any use of the Bible to legitimize or support political options and positions that are based upon injustice, imposed by one person on another, or by one people on another, transform religion into human ideology and strip the Word of God of its holiness, its universality and truth" (2:4).[26] People and non-humans need territory or space in which to reside and flourish. Land, water, and air are homes they all share. In the land, people as custodians are required to live up to the expectation of the laws and remember their previous alien status (Gen 17:8; Exod 23:9) as the expression of God's love and justice to all.

6. What do you think is the New Testament theology of land?

The land belongs to God, who gives it to care-takers who live on the earth to experience God's presence. In situations of landlessness, such as that during the exile, the people were reminded of God's presence and redemption (Isa

26. "A Moment of Truth: A Word of Faith, Hope and Love from the Heart of Palestinian Suffering."

40–60). This "diasporic consciousness" is a key theological ethic of human life in the Bible, what the book of Hebrews called "faith": "All of these died in faith without having received the promises . . . They confessed that they were strangers and foreigners on the earth, for people who speak in this way make it clear that they are seeking a homeland . . . But as it is, they desire a better country, that is, a heavenly one. Therefore, God is not ashamed to be called their God; indeed, he has prepared a city for them" (11:13–16).

Three contributors (Zacharias, García-Johnson, Ramanstwana) focus explicitly on the theme of creation theology, eco-justice, and the crisis of the earth. Besides his essay, García-Johnson also adds, "The Mother Earth (Pachamama) was transformed into 'empty, unutilized, and leaderless' land. The original 'americans,' americans in mestizaje creations and their successors, have become landless. This is a double jeopardy. Ultimately, the land is the earth, alive, a divine messenger and covenant partner of the Spirit of Life . . . Jesus maintained a dynamic relationship with the earth." Zacharias points out that "the dominion mandate as interpreted through the colonial Western lens would be the prime toxic text." He clarifies that, "For the wider Christian community, it is important to recognize that sacralization is not deification. Most Indigenous peoples, and certainly Indigenous followers of Jesus, do not worship the earth."

From a Chinese perspective, I find the implications of this discussion intriguing and necessary. My reading of Genesis 1–2 and Romans 8 has changed after I encountered eco-feminist theology, Chinese Daoist philosophy, and Native American theology.[27] My former professor and colleague, Rosemary Ruether, has shown rightfully the correlation between the oppression of women and exploitation of the earth as a result of the patriarchal interpretation of the Bible.[28]

In both the Genesis and Romans texts, I see God's Spirit permeating human and nonhuman worlds—the Spirit, called "Dao" in Chinese, is the life force that enables the differentiated creatureliness to be interconnected with one another. Dao, as the matrix of creation and medium of organic solidarity, connects heaven, humanity, and all creation. Dao, the life force of the cosmos and its moral fiber/power (*de*), allows humanity

27. Yeo, *Eve, Gaia and God*, 239–88; *Zhuangzi and James*, 281–305. On my previous work on Pauline theology and Native American cultures, see Yeo, "Christ and the Earth in Pauline and Native American Understandings," 179–218.

28. Among her numerous books, see Ruether, *Sexism and God-Talk*, 73; also LaDuke, *All Our Relations*, 75, 98, 101–15.

to participate and lives out the cosmic life of *dao-de* (*logos-virtue*).[29] Similarly, the Lakota people used the phrase "*mitakuye oyasin*" ("all my relations") to refer to the interconnectedness of every member of creation.[30] Both worldviews affirm that the land(scape) provides the materiality for the interconnectedness of all creatures, whereby we all live *together* in solidarity rather than superiority, mutuality rather than hierarchy, interdependence rather than utilitarianism.

Any biblical interpretation that sees humankind as mandated to "subjugate the earth" misses the human vocation to care for nonhuman creation and even their own kind. The "subjected" language in Gen 1:28 and Romans 8:20 has to be interpreted in the semantic context of the power of dominating sin and futility (or destruction). Thus, what is key is the vocation of humanity to be God's instrument to care for the earth in overcoming the chaotic universe and endangered world. The Genesis 1 creation narrative is not so much *ex nihilo* (out of nothing) but *ex tumult* (out of tumult); thus, God's creation is saving and forming goodness out of "formlessness and void" (*tohu wabohu*).

Lubunga W'Ehusha, a professor at the University of KwaZulu-Natal in South Africa, argues for the desperate need to redeem "the priestly role of theology for the land of Africa"; he believes "'radical rethinking' is needed because Western culture has failed to consider humankind as part of the web of life, as depending on, and living in communion with, nonhuman creatures."[31] I also find that The Earth Bible Project articulates this moral obligation of humanity well, especially in its successful attempt to overcome "anthropocentric, patriarchal and androcentric approach to reading the text."[32] I am attracted to its endeavor to construct a hermeneutic that retrieves and empowers the "voice of the Earth."[33] The project affirms six principles to honor and mutually care for the earth (land, sea, air) as our kin: intrinsic worth, interconnectedness, voice, purpose, mutual custodianship, and resistance.[34]

---

29. Yeo, *Musing with Confucius and Paul*, 122–30.

30. Yeo, "Christ and the Earth in Pauline," 202–3.

31. W'Ehusha, "Redeeming the Priestly Role of Theology for the Land of Africa," 305.

32. See Habel et al. eds., *The Earth Bible*, 5 volumes. Here, the Earth Bible Team, "The Voice of Earth," 23.

33. The Earth Bible Team, "The Voice of Earth," 24.

34. The Earth Bible Team, "The Voice of Earth," 22.

Biblical Hermeneutics and Its Ethics

7. How does your paper use "postcolonial" biblical interpretation? Do you find some methods of interpreting the Bible problematic, especially on the theologies of land?

The method of biblical and theological interpretation used in this volume is interdisciplinary. Beyond traditional historical-critical methods, most essays lean heavily on cultural studies, social analysis, and postcolonial hermeneutic. For example, Ramanstwana explains that,

> From a decolonial perspective, we continue to live in a world burdened by the structures of colonialism, which continually pushes Africa into the zone of nonbeing. The hope for Africa will be there when we start thinking outside the confines of Euro-American hegemony and determine the future of Africa in our own pace. My essay focuses on a decolonial approach that pays attention to the power relations between the colonizer and the colonized as it relates to the formation of the biblical canon. Decolonial reading seeks to analyze the nature of the relationship between Israel and the imperial powers who dominated Israel."

Ramanstwana's paper has identified two models discernible in the Hexateuch: 1) the negotiation for land in the territory of the other as projected in the patriarchal narratives (Genesis 12–50); and 2) the conquest model as projected in Exodus–Joshua that provides an example of settler colonialism.

Zacharias, however, clarifies why his essay does not use the term "postcolonial hermeneutic" explicitly: "'Postcolonial hermeneutic' is not often a term used in North America (or Canada at least) since the colonists are still in power. We are not at the point where we are 'post' colonization. I would tend to describe what I do as 'intercultural' or 'decolonizing/decolonized' hermeneutic."

To use de-colonial and postcolonial hermeneutics in re-reading the Bible will unveil new theological loci emerging out of this research that otherwise would be ignored in traditional biblical studies. At the same time, it will expose a lack of critical understanding of terminologies and concepts. Let me give an example.

I used to read Gen 12:1–3 as: "If you bless Israel, God will bless you. If you go against Israel, God will curse you." Twenty years ago, when I visited Bethlehem for the first time, I was told by my Palestinian Christian friend, "Why do you make me, an Arab, the problem in this Israeli–Palestinian conflict?" That hit me hard. I had a naïve and wrong assumption that, "God gave the land to the Jewish people as an eternal possession. The Jews have the divine right to the land." I thought God must be prejudiced, if not racist, but if the Bible described God that way, who was I to question God? I totally mistook Melchizedek to be a pious Jew, a faithful Israelite, not knowing that he was a gentile but a priest of El Elyon (God most high; Gen 14:18–20; Heb 7:10–12).[35]

To use a simple equation regarding the modern State of Israel with biblical Israel is naïve. Genesis 12:1–3 actually reads, "Now the LORD said to Abram, 'Go from your country and your kindred and your father's house to the land that I will show you. . . . I will bless those who bless you, and the one who curses you I will curse; and in you all the families of the earth shall be blessed.'" Theologically, the Abrahamic covenant expresses the calling of Abraham as God's instrument to reach all nations; thus, the exceptionalism of "Israel" (the word is not even in Genesis 12) is absent in this text.[36]

The question of co-existence and difference needs to be asked in light of how we read many of these difficult or even "toxic" texts in the Bible. On the one hand, for example, we fail to note that Abraham and Isaac were in congenial relationships with settled communities in the coastal plains of Canaan, and covenants were made (Gen 21:32–34; 26:28–31). On the other hand, we need to admit that texts such as Deuteronomy 7:2 and the book of Joshua in particular, insist on making no covenants with the locals, or even to destroy these Indigenous Peoples completely. A cross-cultural method that uses postcolonial insights can enable us to re-examine, who are the Hebrews, Israel, and Jews in the OT.[37] Our tendency is to be preoccupied with and to preserve, racial/ethnic purity.[38] This is the universal sin of idolatry of kinship and family.

---

35. Abram (a Hebrew, but neither an Israelite nor a Jew) was from present-day Iraq, and did he ever stop being a "gentile" after his encounter with Elohim and Yahweh? The words such as "Jew" and "Israelite" were not even around at the time of Melchizedek or Abraham.

36. See also Brueggemann, *Chosen?*, 31; Brueggemann, *The Land*, 3–15.

37. Katanacho, *The Land of Christ*, 39–66. See also Brueggemann, *The Land*, 22–28, 69–76.

38. See Bantum, *The Death of Race*, 121–22. In this essay, instead of "race" (referring to physical aspect of skin, hair, eye colors), I prefer to use the category of "ethnicity" (referring to biological and sociological factors such as cultures, ancestry, language, and nationality).

The biblical usage of these terms ("Hebrews," "Israel," and "Jews") is nuancing their meanings as a way of using ambiguity to express the theology that God does not respect the differentiation of skin color, lineage, family, territory, gender, or social class (cf. Gal 3:28). All peoples are called and loved by God equally, and all are created in the image of God.

Yohanna Katanacho, a Palestinian Christian scholar who surveys the use of the word "Israel" in the Bible, notes its broad meanings: 1) it denotes the person Jacob (Gen 32:28); 2) it refers to Jacob's children (Gen 34:7); 3) it symbolizes Jacob's tribes (Gen 47:27), including all the twelve tribes (Exod 1:7), all the tribes but excluding the Reubenites, Gadites, and Manasseh (Josh 22:1–11), or all the tribes but excluding Benjamin (Judg 20:35); 4) during the united Kingdom before the fall of Samaria, the term "Israel" may exclude men of Judah (1 Sam 17:52, 18:16); 5) but after the fall of the Northern Kingdom, Isaiah (56:1–8), Jeremiah, and Ezekiel used "Israel" to refer to followers of Yahweh.[39] It is key that the theological usage (those who believe or follow Yahweh) takes on a far more important meaning than lineage or cultural usage. I interpret this to mean that the Bible is using theology to reorder and fulfill our cultural identities. Of course, this interpretive move is doing biblical theology in an abstract way, similar to our previous affirmation that, all land belongs to God and therefore it needs to be shared with all. I am aware how such interpretive move could be misunderstood, and in fact abused by the colonial impulse to acquire land and then engage in a "civilizing" project of "saving the savage" in the name of "christianizing" their "primitive" cultures and "native" identities.[40] The devastation of such biblical misinterpretation is genocide and ecocide to the Indigenous Peoples who are cut off both from the land, their ancestors, their history and cultures—in sum, their identities annihilated. "Using theology to reorder and fulfill one's cultural identities" in the land issue is not about cultural destruction but empowerment, creative transformation, and meaningful biblical translation.[41]

Such theological usage of one's cultural and theological identities continues into the NT, where the word "Israel" also has multiple meanings: 1) God's people (Matt 2:6); 2) the twelve tribes (Matt 19:28); 3) Jews in Jerusalem (2:22); and 4) Paul's ancestry (*sun-genēs*). But note that, in the last usage,

39. Katanacho, *The Land of Christ*, 39–46.

40. Yeo, "Christ and the Earth in Pauline and Native American," 185–91.

41. See my discussion on a wide range of cross-cultural strategies in *What Has Jerusalem to Do with Beijing?*, 46–52.

Paul makes a critical statement, *"not all* Israelites belong to Israel" (Rom 9:6). As also in Rom 2:28–29, Paul uses theological meaning to ascertain what is "true" Israel or Jew: "For a person is not a Jew who is one outwardly [known/ plain], nor is true circumcision something outward and physical. Rather, a person is a Jew who is one inwardly [hidden], and real circumcision is a matter of the heart—it is in the Spirit and not in the letter."[42]

Land and ethnicity are metaphors used as a means to an end. Land as divine gift is used as a means to the end of covenantal faithfulness between God's presence and the people's responsibility. Imperialism and exceptionalism do not have a place in Christian theology. The theology of God's family is a "radical reordering" of the people (ethnos/ethnicity). Ethnicity in the Bible is a dynamic category used to re-order the relationship with one's familial, cultural, and ancestral grouping by means of one's relationship with God.

Conclusion

In addition to the introductory essay, Walter Brueggemann supplies three broad questions for readers to engage with, as he reminds us of our socio-theological responsibility to the land:

1. How might this urgent social analysis of our work be made more accessible and more public?

2. How might biblical covenant be possible in a world of predatory ideology?

3. What might contribute to an epistemic crisis that emancipates from the killing grind of technological, military consumerism that is endlessly predatory?

The four Majority World and Indigenous theologians suggest that the task is noble and much needed in our age. Zacharias comments on covenant theology saying, "Covenant really is the best way to think about our creation story. Covenant is the way God relates to his creation, and we see the reciprocity of covenant in the creation story—something I tried to

---

42. Likewise, Rev 2:9 ("I know the slander on the part of those who say that they *are Jews and are not,* but are a synagogue of Satan") and Rev 3:9 ("I will make those of the synagogue of Satan who say that they *are Jews and are not,* but are lying").

emphasize. But I think our creation story shows that we are placed in a covenant relationship with the land as well."

Raheb speaks to the "epistemic crisis that emancipates" question as he writes, "We need to realize that a white Anglo-Saxon theology was partly responsible for colonization projects worldwide. We need to give more room to voices from the majority world and minoritized communities, to theologians who experienced land loss and land colonization. That is why this project is important. To employ ideology criticism is now more important than ever."

Ramanstwana thinks of a more practical way to move this project forward: "The book should be made more accessible by making it available electronically as well. When the book becomes available, it may be worthwhile that we have the permission to market it in our respective countries."

Last but not least, García-Johnson offers a few creative thoughts: "Informing the curricula of the imperial-colonized university with a de-colonial theology of the land; having US theological schools working as true partners with Majority World seminaries/universities/Bible schools on practical projects of the land (such as forced displacement in Colombia); creating professional certificates for the laity addressing issues concerning the land, bioregionalism, ecology, theology."

In the end, we find ourselves having more questions than answers, thus we yearn to listen and learn more as we continue the journey to each another and ourselves. We know we are different among ourselves, yet we are in this together with regard to theologies of the land. The conversation has commenced, but the circle is incomplete. We can only count on readers to join us in inviting those voices either absent or minimal in this volume: women, children, nonhuman families, lay persons, the poor, the Indigenous populations in Oceania, Australia, South America, China (over fifty ethnic minority groups), and in other sacred places.[43]

Our conclusion in this chapter is penultimate, we discover, since the crosscurrents of the issue of land are forceful, and there is no end to what we can interrogate. Many of us find ourselves like little children curious about our encounters with the land and its peoples, punctuated by new explorations and ruptured by freshness of theologies of the Majority World and minoritized communities. At least for me for now, the issues of contested land, spatial injustice, homeless and annihilated identity could be mended by a responsible biblical and theological hermeneutic of holding

43. Yeo, "Biblical Interpretation in the Majority World," 131–69.

land as covenantal gift from our Creator. We offer a glimpse of hope that we want to share with our readers. The research and the exchanges in this volume will help our church and society attend to a robust identity of covenantal faithfulness with God via the biblical reality of land, consequently a world to be molded as "a crown of beauty . . . and a royal diadem" in God's hands (Isa 62:3). As the people of God, called to have deep connectedness with the earth and being its good stewards, our sense of place in light of the Bible and theology will enhance human flourishing marked by God's love and justice in the land and its people.

Bibliography

Ateek, Naim. *Justice and Only Justice: A Palestinian Theology of Liberation*. Maryknoll, NY: Orbis, 1989.

Bantum, Brian. *The Death of Race: Building a New Christianity in a Racial World*. Minneapolis: Fortress, 2016.

Berberich, Christine, and Neil Campbell. "Lines of Flight: Unframing Land, Unframing Identity—Two Speculations." In *Land & Identity: Theory, Memory, and Practice*, edited by Christine Berberich et al., 283–304. New York: Rodopi, 2012.

Brueggemann, Walter. *Chosen? Reading the Bible amid the Israeli–Palestinian Conflict*. Louisville: Westminster John Knox, 2015.

———. *The Land: Place as Gift, Promise, and Challenge in Biblical Faith*. 2nd ed. Overtures to Biblical Theology. Minneapolis: Fortress, 2002.

Comer, Krista. *Landscapes of the New West: Gender and Geography in Contemporary Women's Writing*. Chapel Hill: University of North Carolina Press, 1999.

Cunningham, Philip A. "A Catholic Theology of the Land?: The State of the Question." *Studies in Christian-Jewish Relations* 8 (2013) 1–15.

Dawson, Andrew and Nigel Rapport edited. *Migrants of Identity: Perceptions of 'Home' in a World of Movement*. New York: Berg, 1998.

de Vos, J. Cornelis. "'Holy Land' in Joshua 18:1–10." In *The Land of Israel in Bible, History, and Theology: Studies in Honour of Ed Noort*, edited by Jacques van Ruiten and J. Cornelis de Vos, 61–72. Vetus Testamentum Supplements 124. Leiden: Brill, 2009.

Dikötter, Frank. *Mao's Great Famine: The Story of China's Most Devastating Catastrophe*. New York: Bloomsbury, 2016.

The Earth Bible Team. "The Voice of Earth: More than Metaphor?" In *The Earth Story in the Psalms and the Prophets*, edited by Norman C. Habel, 23–28. The Earth Bible 4. Sheffield: Sheffield Academic, 2001.

Farrell, Kirby. "Eschatological Landscape." In *Land & Identity: Theory, Memory, and Practice*, edited by Christine Berberich et al., 117–140. New York: Rodopi, 2012.

Griffin, Susan. *Woman and Nature: The Roaring Inside Her*. Berkeley: Counterpoint, 2016.

Habel, Norman C. et al. edited, *The Earth Bible*. 5 vols. Sheffield: Sheffield Academic, 2000–.

Isaac, Munther. *From Land to Lands, from Eden to the Renewed Earth*. Carlisle, UK: Langham Creative Projects, 2015.

Katanacho, Yohanna. *The Land of Christ: A Palestinian Cry*. Nazareth: Bethlehem Bible College, 2012.

LaDuke, Winona. *All Our Relations: Native Struggles for Land and Life*. Cambridge: South End, 1999.

"A Moment of Truth: A Word of Faith, Hope and Love from the Heart of Palestinian Suffering." In *If Americans Knew*. https://ifamericansknew.org/cur_sit/moment-truth.html.

Patai, Raphael, ed. *The Complete Diaries of Theodor Herzl*. 5 vols. New York: Herzl, 1960.

Patte, Daniel. *Ethics of Biblical Interpretation: A Reevaluation*. Louisville: Westminster John Knox, 1995.

Raheb, Mitri. *I Am a Palestinian Christian*. Minneapolis: Fortress, 1995.

Roy, Arundhati. "The Pandemic is a Portal." *Financial Times* April 3, 2020: https://www.ft.com/content/10d8f5e8-74eb-11ea-95fe-fcd274e920ca Accessed April 22, 2020.

Ruether, Rosemary R. *Sexism and God-Talk*. London: SCM, 1983.

Saltman, Michael. "Introduction." In *Land and Territoriality*, edited by Michael Saltman, 1–18. New York: Berg, 2002.

Soja, Edward W. *Postmodern Geographies*. London: Verso, 1989.

van der Meer, Michaël N. "'Sound the Trumpet!' Redaction and Reception of Joshua 6:2–25." In *The Land of Israel in Bible, History, and Theology: Studies in Honour of Ed Noort*, edited by Jacques van Ruiten and J. Cornelis de Vos, 19–43. Vetus Testamentum Supplements 124. Leiden: Brill, 2009.

W'Ehusha, Lubunga. "Redeeming the Priestly Role of Theology for the Land of Africa." *Old Testament Essays* 27.1 (2014) 302–19.

Wagner, Donald E. *Dying in the Land of Promise: Palestine and Palestinian Christianity from Pentecost to 2000*. London: Melisende, 2003.

Yeo, K. K. "Biblical Interpretation in the Majority World." In *The Oxford History of Protestant Dissenting Traditions*. Vol. 5, *The Twentieth Century Themes and Variations in a Global Context*, edited by Mark Hutchinson, 131–69. Oxford: Oxford University Press, 2018.

———. "Christ and the Earth in Pauline and Native American Understandings." In *Cross-Cultural Paul: Journeys to Others, Journeys to Ourselves*, edited by Charles Cosgrove, Herold Weiss, and K. K. Yeo, 179–218. Grand Rapids: Eerdmans, 2005.

———. *Chairman Mao Meets the Apostle Paul: Christianity, Communism, and the Hope of China*. Grand Rapids: Brazos, 2002.

———. *Eve, Gaia and God* [in Chinese]. Shanghai: Huadong Shifan Daxue, 2008.

———. *Musing with Confucius and Paul: Toward a Chinese Christian Theology*. Eugene, OR: Cascade Books, 2008.

———. *What Has Jerusalem to Do with Beijing? Biblical Interpretation from a Chinese Perspective*. 2nd ed. Contrapunctual Readings of the Bible in World Christianity 2. Eugene, OR: Pickwick Publications, 2018.

———. *Zhuangzi and James* [in Chinese]. Shanghai: Huadong Shifan Daxue VI Horae, 2012.

Index of Names

Jasper, David, 24, 25n78, 35
Jenni, Ernst, 96
Jennings, Willie James, 57, 67
Jezebel, the Sidonian king's daughter, 29
Johnson, Willa M., 118, 129
Johnston, Philip, 18
Johnston, Robert K., 64n58, 67
José, Martí, 52
Juel, Donald H., 96

Karamaga, A., 130
Katanacho, Yohanna, 18, 35, 140n14, 151n37, 152, 156
Katongole, E. M., 136
Khapoya, Vincent B., 100n5, 129
Khoury, Jiries, 16, 35
Khoury, Rafiq, 16, 35
Kickel, Walter, 13n6, 14n17, 35
Kidwell, Clara Sue, 55n36, 80, 96
Kiefer, Jörn, 117n81, 129
Kilroy-Ewbank, Lauren, 58n41, 67
Kinghorn, J., 103n18, 129
Kingsbury, Jack Dean, 96
Kiogora, Timothy G., 109n51, 129
Klappert, Bernhard, 13
Knoppers, Gary N., 115n72, 129-30
Koehler, Ludwig, 74n13, 76, 78n31, 79n36, 85n52, 96
König, A., 129
Koschorke, Klaus, 41n7, 67
Kratz, Reinhard G., 114n71, 129
Kretzshmar, Louise, 129
Kürshcner-Pelkmann, F., 130
Kwok, Pui-Ian, 17, 35

LaDuke, Winona, 148n28, 156
Lalitha, Jayachitra, 67
Landman, W. A., 104n18, 129
Lemche, Niels Peter, 16n41, 35
Levenson, Jon, 17
Levin, C., 131
Levinson, Bernard M., 129
Liew, Tat-siong Benny, 33, 35
Lindberg, Tracey, 129
Lipschits, O., 130
Littell, Franklin, 13
Loden, Lisa, 18n51, 36

Maimela, Simon, 106, 108n42, 129
Mair, John, 41
Maluleke, Tinyiko S., 100, 106n33, 108, 111n58, 129
Mamdani, Mahmood, 103n17, 129
Maritain, Jacques, 103n17, 129
Markmann, C. L., 128
Marquardt, Friedrich Wilhelm, 13, 35
Martin, Oren R., 71n7, 96
Marzal, Manuel M., 67
Masalha, Nur, 22, 24n77, 35
Masenya, Madipoane (Ngwan'a Mphahlele), 126
Mathews, Kenneth A., 74n14, 79n34, 96
Matondi, Prosper B., 102n10, 129
Mbenga, Bernard, 128
McKeown, James, 79n34, 96
Medina, Néstor, 41n6, 42n8, 66-67
Mendenhall, George E, 12
Mignolo, Walter D., 43-45, 46n18, 49, 58n39, 59, 67
Miller, Robert J., 101n8, 129
Mkodzongi, G., 102n12, 129
Mofokeng, Takatso A., 106-7, 129
Moltmann, Jürgen, 71n6, 96
Moo, Douglas J., 70n3, 96
Moo, Jonathan A., 70n3, 96
Moore, Stephen D., 66
Moraña, Mabel, 66
Mosala, Itumeleng, 99, 106, 108, 110-11, 130
Moses, A. D., 131
Moxnes, Halvor, 20, 35-36
Moyo, Sam, 102n12, 130
Mtshiselwa, Ndikho, 126
Mugambi, Jesse N. K., 111, 112n62, 113, 128, 130
Munayer, Salim, 18, 36
Mussner, Franz, 14

Newsom, Carol A., 85n54, 97
Noley, Homer, 80, 96
Noth, Martin, 12
Ntreh, Benjamin A., 126

Olley, John W., 88n58, 97
Omari, C. K., 130

Index of Subjects

Index of Scripture